YOU can Make a Difference

yOU can Make a Difference

Tony Campolo

WORD PUBLISHING

Word (UK) Ltd
Milton Keynes, England

WORD AUSTRALIA
Heathmont, Victoria, Australia
STRUIK CHRISTIAN BOOKS (PTY) LTD
Salt River, South Africa
ALBY COMMERCIAL ENTERPRISES PTE LTD
Balmoral Road, Singapore
CONCORDE DISTRIBUTORS LTD
Havelock North, New Zealand
JENSCO LTD
Hong Kong
SALVATION BOOK CENTRE
Malaysia

YOU CAN MAKE A DIFFERENCE

Copyright © 1984 by Anthony Campolo

First published in the USA by Word Books, Waco, Texas

First UK edition 1985

ISBN 0-85009-056-3

All Scripture quotations, unless otherwise identified, are from the Authorized Version of the Bible. The quotation marked by NIV is from The New International Version, © 1978 by the New York International Bible Society, used by permission.

Anglicization & typesetting by Nuprint Services Ltd.

Printed in Great Britain for WORD (UK) LTD by Cox & Wyman Ltd, Reading.

90   91   92   93   /   10   9   8

Contents

To my big sisters
ROSE and ANN
who taught me how to have fun

'It is tempting to describe the author as being larger than life. But life for Tony Campolo seems larger than anything else. What he says is what he is. That makes him and this book very special indeed.'

Peter Meadows

COMMITMENT
Getting Beyond Good Intentions

1

What is commitment?

I teach at a small, church-related college in the USA, near Philadelphia called Eastern College. Every May students come into my office, sit down, look at me across the desk, and say something like this, 'Doc, I'm not coming back next term.'

I whip off my glasses, peer near-sightedly at them and try to look professional. 'Pray tell,' I say. 'Why?' They always look back at me with a strained look and say, 'I need time, Doc, I need time.' I say to myself, 'This guy's done nothing for the past six months – and now he needs time?'

I know what he is going to say next. He's going to say, 'I need time to find myself.' There is a whole generation out there trying to find themselves, and they all look in the same place: Boulder, Colorado.

Then it gets real strange in a hurry. The student says, 'Doc, Doc, I'm tired of playing all these roles that society says I have to play. I'm tired of being the me that my friends expect me to be, the me that the church expects me to be, the me that my parents expect me to be. I've got to peel away each of these socially prescribed identities. I've got to peel away each of these socially constructed roles. I've got to peel them away – do you hear? – and come to grips with the core of my being, the essence of my personality!'

To all of this I have a simple retort: 'Look, suppose after you peel away each of these socially prescribed identities, after you peel away each of these socially created selves, you discover you are an onion! Now, *that* is a *real* possibility. You peel away all of the skins of the onion, what's left? Nothing. The onion is nothing more than the sum total of its skins.'

It just may be that the human personality is nothing more than the sum total of all the roles society has trained him or her to play. That is, after someone has peeled away each of the socially generated selves and takes prolonged journey into their inner self, and gets there, they will discover, 'Hey, nobody's at home!' Now that's a real possibility.

You see, there is a comon presupposition that everybody has a 'self' waiting to be found. I don't believe that. I don't believe that there is an essential self waiting to be found through introspection. If there were, somebody would have found it long ago. Of the thousands of young people who have taken time off to find themselves, you would think that somebody would eventually come back and say, 'Doc, Doc, I found myself just north of Cleveland!' But it never happens.

That's because there is no such thing as a self waiting to be found. Quite to the contrary, the self is something waiting to be created. And there is only one way to create a self; there is only one way to create an identity; there is only one way to create meaning in life; and that, friends, is through commitment. Only through commitment do people achieve an identity and a meaning and a purpose in life. And there are very few committed people in this world.

As a matter of fact, one of the few places I see committed people is in airports. That's funny, you say, committed people in the airports? Of course I'm referring to the Hari Krishna people. I like them, but they are strange! I fly in and out of the Philadelphia airport a lot and I've got to know some of the ones who hang out there. Since I know them, I usually can get to them before they get to me. I usually sneak up on their blind side, grab them, spin them around, kiss them on the cheek, and say, 'Jesus loves you!' It blows them away. I don't win many converts that way, but it's lots of fun. However, there's one thing I have to say about the followers of Hari Krishna: they are committed people. Consequently, they are people who have an identity, a clear definition of selfhood and a well-established meaning to life. Their only problem is that their god isn't real and they are deceived.

Real commitment

Today you are being called to commit your life to Jesus Christ. He *is* real. He's every bit as real as you are. He is with you at this very moment. He wants you to establish your identity in Him. He wants you to create your purpose for life in service to His cause. He calls you to define who you are by understanding what He has called you to become. You are determined by your commitment, and you *are* a Christian if you have committed your life to Jesus.

One of my favourite stories describing commitment is about a tightrope walker named Blondin. In the late 1890s he strung a tightrope across Niagara Falls, and then before ten thousand screaming people, inched his way from the Canadian side of the falls to the USA side. When he got there, the crowd began shouting his name, 'Blondin! Blondin! Blondin! Blondin!'

Finally he raised his arms, quietened the crowd and (how's this for an ego trip?) shouted to them, 'I am Blondin! Do you believe in me?' The crowd shouted back, 'We believe! We believe! We believe!'

Again he quietened the crowd and once more he shouted to them, 'I'm going back across the tightrope but this time I'm going to carry someone on my back. Do you believe I can do that?' The crowd yelled, 'We believe! We believe!'

He quietened them one more time and then he said, 'Who will be that person?' The crowd went dead. Nothing.

Finally, out of the crowd stepped one man. He climbed on Blondin's shoulders and for the next three and a half hours, Blondin inched his way back across the tightrope to the Canadian side of the falls.

The point of the story is blatantly clear: ten thousand people stood there that day chanting, 'We believe, we believe!' but only one person really believed. Believing is not just saying, 'I accept the facts.' Believing is giving your life over into the hands of the one in whom you say you believe. Believing is a commitment.

The most serious problem with the church today is that while it is filled with believers, it is seriously devoid of committed disciples. Oh, everybody believes. Everywhere I go, I find believers. As I travel from one end of the USA to the other, I find a nation with almost a hundred million people who call themselves 'born again.' But I wonder how many of them are committed. I wonder what Jesus really means to them.

You could go down to a local bar and nudge the guy next to you and ask, 'Do you believe in Jesus?' In all probability, he would say that he does believe in Jesus. He may be half bombed as he sits at the bar, but he still believes in Jesus. If you asked him theological questions, his answers would probably sound as evangelical as any you have ever heard. But that does not make him a Christian. That's because the thing that makes a person a Christian is not believing the right stuff, but whether or not that person is committed to Jesus. Being a Christian is dependent upon a person's turning over his or her life to Jesus so that Jesus can use that person to do the things He wants to do in this world. A person is a Christian when he or she becomes totally committed to changing the things that God wants changed.

Are you committed? That's the big question. Are you willing to do whatever Jesus wants you to do? Are you willing to be whatever Jesus wants you to be? Are you willing to go wherever Jesus wants you to go? Jesus offers no 'cheap grace.' He does not call you to be a nice believer. He calls you to committed discipleship.

Being what Jesus would be

When I was a kid, I read a book by an author named Sheldon. The book is called *In His Steps*. It has a simple premise: To be a Christian is to *commit* yourself to do whatever Jesus would do if He were in your shoes; to act as Jesus would act if He were in your place; to make the decisions Jesus would make if He were faced with your options. The book moved me as I read it and I decided to commit myself to Christ as Sheldon suggested. I decided to do whatever Jesus would do if Jesus were in my shoes. That was going to be my thing from that moment on. Whatever He'd do, I'd do. I was committed.

The day after making that decision, I went to my secondary school, West Philadelphia High. It was a great school, and our class had the best room for registration in the whole school, room 48! Room 48 was where the 'jocks' were assigned. And I was what we called a 'jock'. Now a jock is a student who's 'thick' and just likes playing sports. But there's more to being a jock than simply being an athlete. Athletes may play sports, but jocks have style. You can always tell a real jock. A jock doesn't just walk, a jock *moves*. You have to be cool to be a jock. A jock is the kind of guy who *moves* along the corridors at school and expects the girls to line up along the walls and sing, 'How Great Thou Art.'

All the jocks were in Room 48. The football players, the basketball players, the wrestlers. But in addition to the jocks and superstars, there were also four kids who didn't belong. They were the members of the chess team. Now don't get me wrong – not all chess-players are like these guys, but the chess team at West Philadelphia High that year was made up of 'wimps.' If that word doesn't communicate, let's try 'nerds.' You know the kind of kids I'm talking about. I'm describing the kind of kid who, on a rainy day, comes to school wearing *galoshes*. Or brings his lunch in a brown paper bag – and saves the bag!

As I coolly *moved* into our classroom, an urgent but simple question came to me: 'If Jesus was in my shoes, where would He sit? If Jesus was in my place who would He choose for a friend?' Would He sit with the superstars, and the jocks? Would He choose to be with the 'in' kids? Would He choose to identify with the popular kids? Or would Jesus go over and become a friend of the 'wimps?'

It didn't take me long to resolve that line of questioning. Having read the Scriptures and learned about Jesus, I knew exactly what He would do. Jesus would have been a friend of the friendless. He would have sat with some wimp. I decided to do what He would do, so I went over and sat next to one. Strangely enough, we became friends and we stayed friends that entire year, right up until we left.

Now I really wish this story had one of those storybook endings. I wish I could tell you, 'Because I *loved* that wimp, because I *gave* myself to that wimp, because I *cared* for that wimp, that wimp *blossomed*! He became a *wholesome, powerful, dynamic* personality. And *today*, my friends, that wimp is *Ronald Reagan!*' I really wish this story had one of those happy surprise 'success story' endings! Actually, in this particular case, the wimp stayed a wimp. As a matter of fact, I saw him in New York a year ago and he's still a wimp.

Religious stories don't always turn out to have glorious and wonderful endings. If you are going to follow Jesus, you do the things that Jesus would do without being concerned about how everything will turn out. You learn that there is joy in being faithful to what He requires of you, regardless of the results.

Doing what Jesus would do is at the very core of the Christian lifestyle. To be a follower of Christ means asking yourself every moment of every day, 'How would Jesus act if He were in my shoes – in my situation?' To be a Christian is to live out life as Jesus would live it regardless of how tough such a commitment proves to be.

When you start trying to be what Jesus would be, when you start trying to do what Jesus would do, you are going to discover that you are committed to a lifestyle that is tougher than anything else you've ever tried to do. Living the Christian life is incredibly difficult. In fact, when you try to imitate Jesus for any length of time, you'll discover that you don't have what it takes. You will find that in your attempt to do what Jesus would do if He was in your shoes, you will fail over and over again.

In my early days as a Christian, I failed day after day after day. I'd say, 'God, I did these things wrong,' and I would list all the ways I'd failed to do what Jesus would do and be what Jesus would be. Then I'd add, 'Lord, tomorrow I'm going to do better.'

Then I'd go out the next day and usually do exactly those things that I had told God I wouldn't do the night before. And at the end of the day I'd get down and confess my shortcomings again. But I would fail over and over again. It would go on and on like that.

It got to the point where I just felt like praying 'ditto' each night.

In more recent years, I have learnt the reason for my continual failures. I have learnt that there's a big difference between my trying to live for Jesus and allowing Jesus to live through me. Let me put it another way. There's a big difference between my trying to do something for Him and His trying to do something *through* me. Got that?

You see, what Jesus wants to do is to come into my life and into your life and help us to live out His will. He doesn't simply ask us to do what He would do! He offers to come in and possess us so that He can enable us to do what we could never do ourselves. This is a crucial fact to remember. If each of us allows God to possess us and strengthen us, He will give to each of us the ability to do His will. Without Him neither you nor I can live the life He wants us to live.

When I was a jock at school, I did both track and field events. I wasn't great, but I was OK. One day my coach took the whole team to Franklin Field in Philadelphia to see the great Roger Bannister run a race. He was the first man to run the mile in less than four minutes, and we were all anxious to see if he could do it again.

Our entire team was standing and cheering as the world's greatest runners readied themselves for the final event of the meet, the mile run. I can remember the excitement as the race got under way. All the runners remained bunched together for the first three laps. Then on the last lap, Bannister pulled away from the pack. The crowd went crazy as he picked up the pace and distanced himself from the other runners. Everyone in the stands knew he was going to do it again. The four-minute mile barrier was about to be shattered again. When he crossed the finish line, the crowd exploded. People were screaming and jumping up and down. We all went bananas when they announced that Bannister had run another sub-four-minute mile.

But while we were all cheering, I happened to look down. I saw Roger Bannister collapse in exhaustion. After crossing the finish line he just passed out. A first aid team hurried on to the field with a stretcher. They loaded Bannister on it and quickly carried him off the field.

And as they were carrying a 'half-dead' Roger Bannister to the emergency room, my coach put his hand on my shoulder and said, 'Tony, you're our miler. I expect you to do that.' At that moment, as I saw Bannister's exhausted form disappear under the stands, two things went through my mind. Number one, I didn't know whether I ever *could* do that. I liked to run and I was a jock, but to be a great miler, to run the mile in less than four minutes, that was something else again. No way could I do it. I lacked the ability, I lacked the build.

Secondly, in addition to lacking the physical ability, I also lacked the will. I would have liked to have been a great runner, but not badly enough to risk dropping dead for old West Philly High.

It's the same with living like Jesus. Like you, I lack both ability and will to carry it off. There is an absence of the will-power necessary to stick with our commitments to Christ. Secondly, there is an inability to do in our own strength what we know God wants us to do.

But here's the good news of the gospel: when you and I allow Jesus to come in and possess us, He enables us to will what neither of us could ever will before – He enables us to do what neither of us could ever do before. The Scripture says, 'For it is God which worketh in you both to *will* and to *do* of His good pleasure.'

What I want you to get is this. First, you must become committed to Jesus, and not just simply believe in Him. You must commit yourself to Him and say, 'Jesus I'm Yours, I'm going to do whatever You want me to. I'm going to live the way You want me to live every moment of every day. I will try to imitate what You would do if You were in my shoes.' Secondly, you must say to Jesus, 'I want You to come into my life and possess me and enable me to do what I could never do on my own; to will what I could never will before; to live as I could never live in my own strength.'

A life of joy

Here's some more good news: when you are committed to Jesus, when Jesus comes in and possesses you, you are going to know joy. In fact, you are going to know joy like you've never, ever known joy before. It will undoubtedly blow you away.

When Jesus takes total possession of you – when you are surrendered to Him – your life is marked by a spontaneous joy that makes you into a fun person. My two kids often say to me, 'Dad, you are a nice guy but you are dangerous.' I can appreciate that, and even agree with it. I know that the Spirit of God has created in me an aliveness that is hard to contain.

For instance, I become dangerous in lifts. Society has trained us to behave in certain ways when we get into lifts, particularly crowded lifts. If you get into a crowded lift you are supposed to turn and face the door. However, I have discovered that there is a great deal of fun in just getting into a crowded lift and not turning. Face to face with other people, I like to say, 'You are probably wondering why I called this meeting, aren't you?' That usually blows them away!

Near our home in Philadelphia there is a toll bridge that crosses the Delaware River. The toll on the bridge is twenty-five cents, but sometimes when I cross the bridge I give the toll-collector fifty cents and I tell him, 'Twenty-five cents are for me and the other twenty-five are for my good friend who is in the car right behind me.' I don't know who is in the car behind me, but I want to tell you that it is worth twenty-five cents just to pull away from the toll-booth, look in the rear view mirror and watch the toll-collector trying to explain it to the guy in the next car.

Whenever I talk about these things people ask what it's got to do with being a Christian and I must respond to such a question by saying, 'Everything!' Being possessed by Jesus creates a spontaneity and a joy that sends you bursting forth into the world as a fun person. That is why I tell you as young people that giving your life to Christ will prove to be the best move you could possibly make. It doesn't curtail your joy and spontaneity. Instead, in your surrender to Christ you will find yourself possessed with a spirit of life that will make you a joy to everyone.

You know, that's not bad theology. I believe that

God is a God of laughter, a God of fun, a God of joy. I want to make this next point very, very clear: If I didn't believe that your life would be overwhelmingly filled with joy in surrendering to Jesus, I wouldn't invite you to do it. I would not ask you to surrender your life to Jesus unless I was convinced that you would be filled with joy in a way that you cannot possibly imagine right now. The presence of Jesus in your life – the result of being totally committed to Him and His will – will make you into a person who knows joy, joy, joy, unspeakable joy.

There's a Pentecostal College near Eastern College where I teach. I'm not Pentecostal, but I talk so fast that I think they think I'm speaking in tongues, so it works out OK. One day they invited me to speak at a chapel service. I like speaking there because they are dynamic, happy people and I enjoy being with them.

Just before I spoke, eight guys took me into a back room of the chapel and got me down on my knees. Then they laid their hands on my head and prayed for me. That was good. I need all the prayer I can get.

There was only one problem. Those guys prayed a long time. And that's usually OK, too. But the longer they prayed, the more tired they got. And the more tired they got, the more they leaned on my head. I want to tell you that when eight guys are leaning on your head, it doesn't feel so good.

One guy wasn't even praying for me. Instead he went on and on praying for somebody named Charlie Stoltzfus. 'Dear Lord,' he shouted, 'You know Charlie Stoltzfus. He lives in that silver caravan about a mile down the road. You know the caravan, Lord, just down the road on the right-hand side.' I felt like saying, 'Come on, knock it off, what do you think God's doing? Saying, "What's the address again?"'

Anyway, he went on and on and on: 'Lord, Charlie told me this morning that he's decided to leave his wife and three kids. He told me that he was walking out on his family. Lord, step in, do something, bring the people in that family back together again!'

All the while, I'm kneeling there with eight guys leaning on my head and I'm asking myself, 'When's this guy going to knock off so I can get these Pentecostal preachers off my head?' But he kept going on and on about Charlie Stoltzfus' leaving his wife and kids, giving God constant reminders that he lived in a silver caravan a mile down the road on the right-hand side.

Finally, the prayers were over and I went into the pulpit and preached. After I was finished, I got in my car, drove to the Pennsylvania motorway, and headed for home.

As I drove onto the motorway, I noticed a hitch-hiker. Now, I know you're not supposed to pick them up, but I'm a preacher and whenever I can get anybody locked in as a captive audience, I do it. So, I stopped and picked him up. We drove a few minutes and I said, 'Hi, my name's Tony Campolo. What's your name?' He said, 'My name is Charlie Stoltzfus.' I couldn't believe it!

I got off the motorway at the next exit and headed back. He got a bit uneasy with that and after a few minutes he said, 'Hey, mister, where are you taking me?' I said, 'I'm taking you *home*.' He narrowed his eyes and asked, 'Why?'

I said, 'Because you just left your wife and three

children, right?' That blew him away. 'Yeah! Yeah, that's right.' With shock written all over his face, he plastered himself against the car door and never took his eyes off me.

I drove off the motorway at the next exit. Then I really did him in as I drove right to his silver caravan. When I pulled up, his eyes seemed to bulge as he asked, 'How did you know that I lived here?' I said, *'God told me.'* (I believe God did tell me.)

We got out of the car and I ordered him to get in that caravan. Half shaking he answered, 'Right mister, sure! Sure! I'm going.'

When he opened the trailer door his wife exclaimed, 'You're back! You're back!' He whispered in her ear and the more he talked, the bigger her eyes got.

Then I said with real authority, 'The two of you sit down. I'm going to talk and you two are going to listen!' Man! Did they listen! I mean, it was as if I was a sort of guru!

That afternoon I led those two young people to Jesus Christ. And today, that guy is a preacher of the gospel out in California.

You're thinking, 'Hey, is being surrendered to Jesus all that wonderful? Is it all that filled with joy?' Please understand this: there is no greater joy than the joy that comes when you sense your life under the control of the Spirit of God. Then you know you are going to be used to do fantastic and wonderful things for God. There's nothing in the world like the joy that comes in being committed to Jesus and being possessed by Him – so that through you He can begin to do the things He would do if He were physically present on the earth in your shoes.

25

The way of suffering

There's a lot of joy to the Christian life. But I don't want you to get the idea that it's all joy. There's also sorrow and suffering in following Jesus. The apostle Paul once prayed, '...that I may know him, and the power of his resurrection, and the fellowship of his sufferings.' Most of us are willing to buy into the joyful experiences when we are possessed by His power, but we have to understand that there is no ecstasy unless we are willing to also experience His agony.

When you become a Christian and when Jesus Christ possesses you, one of the results will be that your heart will be broken by the things that break the heart of Jesus. The things that make Jesus cry will make you cry.

At Eastern College where I teach, I head up the sociology department. Each January we take students to the Dominican Republic and Haiti. I want my students to visit those places because I want them to see what Jesus sees. I want them to feel what Jesus feels. I want their hearts to be broken by the things that break Jesus' heart.

I remember one time when we were in Port-au-Prince, the capital city of Haiti, and a little boy came crawling towards me on the pavement. He was crippled, not because he had been born crippled, but because as an infant his parents deliberately broke his arms and legs and made him into a cripple. His parents thought that a crippled child could collect more money begging from tourists than a child who was whole.

26

I grant you that this boy was an unusual case. But what happened to him was an expression of the cruelty that accompanies extreme poverty. It is an example of the things that break the heart of Jesus.

Some of my students and colleagues at Eastern College have got together and started a feeding programme in the city of Cap-Haitien, Haiti. We're trying to raise enough money to pay for feeding the many suffering children of that miserable city. So far we are able to feed only five hundred children. There are hundreds more in that city who are malnourished. There are tens of thousands in Haiti who are close to death. You know the job I want my college students to do down there? I don't want to give them the job of giving out the food; that's too easy. I would like to put them at the entrance to our feeding centre and tell them that their job is to count the first five hundred children who come in and then say to the others, 'Sorry. No more food. Go on, leave.'

How would you handle that? Could you look a starving Haitian child in the face and say, 'I'm sorry, but you have to starve because we've run out of food'?

I don't want to put a guilt trip on you, but there is something wrong with us when we can spend so much on ourselves, and be so insensitive to the fact that there are five hundred million children in the world today who are suffering from hunger and malnutrition.

When you become possessed by Jesus, when the mind of Christ takes over your mind, when you begin to think His thoughts, when you start to feel what He feels, you will enter into His sufferings. Then the things that break the heart of Jesus will break your heart.

There is an incredible slum area I wish you could visit. It is like thousands of such slums throughout the Third World. It is only a hundred acres in size, yet forty thousand people are squeezed into it. They live in squalor that defies imagination. There is suffering and death everywhere. Amidst those suffering people is a priest who trys to serve them with a dedication worthy of sainthood. One morning that priest woke me and my students at six in the morning. He said, 'I want you to see something.' We followed him through the mud paths that separated the lean-to shacks of that hell-hole. There was a flu epidemic in progress. When flu hits our Western communities, our children miss school. In an improverished Third World country, when malnourished children get the flu, they die. As we made our way through the mud paths of that slum we saw mothers come out of those shacks carrying in their arms the tiny corpses of children who had died during the night. We followed those mothers as they walked with their priest to the edge of the slum where we dug a ditch. And into that ditch we laid the emaciated bodies of those tiny babies, side by side. We heard the mothers scream and cry as only bereaved mothers can scream and cry. The priest said what he had to say and ended with a prayer.

Then we began to shovel the dirt over those tiny dead bodies. As I looked across the ditch, I noticed one of my students, a great big basketball player. I had never seen him cry before, but his lower lip was trembling, his fists were clenched, and tears were running down his cheeks. Something inside of me said, 'Blessed are they that mourn, for they shall be comforted.' Indeed, there is a comfort that is only for those who enter into the sufferings of Jesus.

There is joy in this walk with Jesus, but there is agony, too. To be possessed by Jesus is to begin to care about people like you have never, ever cared for them before. Their hurts will become your hurts, and their agonies will become your agonies, because that's what it means to be in Jesus and to have Jesus in you.

He will not only strengthen you to do His will, He will change your emotional make-up so that you will begin to feel His feelings.

You don't have to go across the sea to find hurting people. You can find them right in your own back yard. One day when I was in my office, my mother called. I'm a good Italian boy and when an Italian mother calls, the Italian boy listens. Mum had some bad news: Mrs Kilpatrick had died. She was a dear, wonderful woman who had lived on my street in West Philadelphia. She had done so many beautiful things for me when I was growing up, like taking me to art museums and concerts. Actually, she had almost single-handedly helped to broaden my cultural horizons. My mother said, 'The least you can do is show some respect and go to the funeral.' So I went. Italians are big on respect.

The next day, I got into the car, drove to the funeral parlour and arrived right at two o'clock. I bounded up the steps, ran inside, took a deep breath, sat down, and bowed my head in prayer. When I lifted my head and looked around, I realized that other than the elderly lady to my immediate left, there wasn't anybody else in the whole room. I peered over the edge of the coffin and I knew that the man in that box did not look like Mrs Kilpatrick. Then I realized that I was at the wrong funeral.

I was just about to make my move and get out when the old woman grabbed my arm. Then she looked at me painfully and said, 'You were his friend, weren't you?' What would you do? Come on now, what would you say? 'No, I didn't know your husband. I wandered in here by accident. Your husband didn't have any friends!'

No way! You couldn't do that and neither could I. I hate to admit this, but for the records I've got to tell you. I lied. I said, 'Yeah, he was a good man. Everybody liked him,' or something like that. I went through the entire funeral with that old woman. It was just the two of us. And after the funeral, we went out to the cemetery, which seemed like a hundred miles away. I stood at the edge of the grave and watched as the coffin was lowered into the grave. In the East we always throw a flower on the coffin. So she threw her flower, and I threw mine.

We got back in the limousine and headed back for town. As we neared the funeral parlour, I said, 'Mrs King, there's something I've got to tell you. I want to be your friend and we can't have a friendship unless I tell the truth. I'm afraid I have to tell you that I really didn't know your husband. I came to his funeral by accident.' She took hold of my hand and squeezed it so tightly it hurt. Then she said slowly, 'You'll never, ever, ever know how much your being with me today meant to me.'

And on the way home, I realized I had done

something of great significance. At first I couldn't
figure out what it was. I hadn't witnessed to her or
given her the Four Spiritual Laws. I hadn't given her
a tract or a Gospel of John. Then this verse came to
me. 'Bear ye one another's burdens, and so fulfil the
law of Christ.'

When you become a Christian, you will develop a
sensitivity to people who are hurting. You will want
to share the hurts of those who suffer. You will know
not only the joy of Jesus, but you will also know the
sorrow that Jesus knows.

Anger at injustice

There is one last thing that you will come to know in
being surrendered to Jesus. You will come to know
His anger. That's right – *anger*. Jesus gets angry.
There are all kinds of things that make Him angry.
Poverty makes Him angry; political oppression makes
Him angry; economic injustice makes Him angry;
racism and sexism makes Him angry. All of these
demonic social conditions make Him angry. It is
time for you to realize that when you become a
Christian, the things that are wrong with this world
will make you angry, too. They will anger you so
much that you will say, 'Jesus, I am ready to join
with You in trying to destroy the works of the devil.'
That's what it says in 1 John 3:8 – we are called to
destroy the works of Satan.

Racism is one of the ugliest works of Satan. Racism
has resulted in hatred between some black and white
people. That is the work of Satan. And when racism
manifests itself, Jesus calls His disciples to anger.

I have a friend by the name of Clarence Jordan.
Actually he's dead now, but I talk about him as still
being a friend because I believe that even though he
is dead, he is more alive today than he has ever been.
Clarence once described going to a church to conduct
a revival meeting in the back hills of South Carolina.
This was back in the mid-1950s, when segregation
was practised and racism was all too common in that
region.

When he took his place behind the pulpit to preach
his first sermon, Clarence looked over the crowd and,
much to his surprise, the congregation was made up
of a mixture of black and white folks. He couldn't
believe what his eyes saw. He wondered how such a
thing could happen.

Following the service, he asked the old hillbilly
preacher who was the pastor of the church, 'How did
you get this way?' The old hillbilly preacher
answered, 'What way?' Clarence said, 'You know,
integrated. Blacks and whites together. Has this come
about because of the Supreme Court decision on
integration?' The old preacher said, 'Supreme Court?
What's the Supreme Court got to do with Christians?'

Good question. Maybe the people of the world
need the Supreme Court to tell them that discrimina-
tion is wrong. But the Bible has already spoken to
Christians on such matters.

'Come on!' said Clarence. 'You know you've got a
weird church here. How did you get it to be this
way?'

'Well,' said the preacher, 'they used to have about
twenty members in this church when the last preacher
died.'

'But there are hundreds and hundreds of people out there now,' Clarence said. 'That's right,' agreed the preacher. 'When that old preacher died, they couldn't get a new preacher no how. So, after about two months, I told the deacons that I'd be the new preacher. Since they didn't have anybody else, they let me preach.'

'I got up the next Sunday, opened the Bible, put my finger down and landed on that verse that says, 'In Christ there is neither Jew nor Greek, bond nor free, male nor female...all are one in Christ Jesus.' So I preached on that,' the old preacher said. 'I told them people how Jesus makes all kinds of people one. When I finished the deacons told me they wanted to talk to me in the back room. And when the deacons got there, they told me they didn't want to hear that kind of preaching no more.'

Clarence asked, 'What did you do then?'

The old hillbilly said, 'I *fired* them deacons. I mean if a deacon's not going to "deke," he ought to be fired.'

Clarence was amazed. 'How come the deacons didn't fire you?'

'They never hired me,' replied the preacher. 'You know, once I found out what bothered them people, I gave it to them every week; I put the knife in the same place, Sunday after Sunday.'

Clarence said, 'Did they put up with it?'

'Not really,' the preacher answered. 'I preached that church down to four people. Sometimes revival begins not when we get a lot of new people into the church, but when we get some of the old people out of the church. If people are going to stand in the way of

33

the moving of God, it's better they be gone. After that we only let Christians in this church.'

'How can you tell who the Christians are?' Clarence wanted to know.

'Well,' answered that old preacher, 'down here we're taught since we're knee-high to a grasshopper that there's a difference between black folk and white folk and they shouldn't mix. But we know that when people get saved then all of that garbage is gone. We know that we got Christians on our hands when all that stuff about race is taken out of folk's hearts. Well, when we got some Christians in this church, it started to grow and grow. And that's how we got to the way we are now.'

That evening, Clarence Jordan went to spend the night at the home of a member of the church. That member was a graduate of Yale with a Ph.D. in English literature who was on the faculty at the University of South Carolina. The man drove seventy miles to go to that church. That night Clarence asked that young, sophisticated member of the intelligent-sia, 'Why do you go to that church? Why do you go to hear that old hillbilly preach? You're used to good English and that preacher can't utter a sentence without making a grammatical error.'

The man answered sternly, 'Sir, I go to that church because that man preaches the gospel.'

The gospel is not simply that you go to heaven when you die; the gospel is much more than that. The gospel is that Jesus is here and now and He will enter into your life and He will remove a lot of things from your consciousness that this culture has bred into you. The gospel will make you love people you've never loved before. This is what that hillbilly preacher knew, which a lot of people who think they are Christians have never learnt.

When you become a Christian, Jesus will invade your life and make you into somebody He can use to change the world. Through you, He will challenge racism. Through you, Jesus will attack sexism, poverty and militarism. That was never taught to me when I was growing up. I never heard that I could be an instrument that God could use to change the world. All I was told was that being a Christian meant I would go to heaven when I died. I was never told that the primary reason Jesus saved me was to make me into somebody whom He could use to change the world into the kind of world He willed for it to be when He created it. I was never told that Christians are called to be angry with the injustices which anger God.

I must admit that Christianity may make you into an angry young woman or an angry young man. That's because you will find intolerable, many of the things that people around you all too readily accept. Little by little, God will change you into an agent of His revolution in history. I know what you are thinking: 'Hey Tony! That's a *big* world out there. Little folks like us can't change it.' If you think that, you're wrong. We *can* change it. God wants to equip us to do it.

I want you to dream dreams, I want you to have visions, I want you to believe that this same Jesus who died on the cross for your sins two thousand years ago is with you right now. I want you to know that He wants to invade your life, that He wants to

35

take possession of you, that He wants to use you to do His will. He truly wants to do this – He wants to use you to touch the lives of people who are hurt, to bring joy to people who are sad. He wants to make you into an agent fighting for His great revolution. He wants to begin to change the world through you.

And when you accept Jesus into your life, things will begin to happen on a scale that will surprise you. You, like the 'Man from la Mancha,' will 'dream the impossible dream.' You will 'fight the unbeatable foe.' You will fight with your 'last ounce of courage.' You will go 'where the brave dare not go.'

God wants to do great things through you. I don't want you just to believe in Him; I want you to be committed to Him. I want you to be ready to say, 'Jesus, I'm ready to do what You would do if You were in my shoes. Come into my life and empower me to do it. I want to know your joy. I want to experience your sorrows. I want to feel your anger. I want to be a person through whom You can express your love to a world that needs You.'

Young person, the world needs you. And Jesus needs you. Jesus calls you to do His work in His world. Now. today. For ever!

VOCATION

*Setting a Course and
Travelling Light*

2

Your part in God's revolution

During the 1960s, one of the most popular singing groups was the Kingston Trio. They had a hit song that went like this:

> They're rioting in Africa.
> They're starving in Spain.
> There's hurricanes in Florida,
>   and Texas needs rain.
> The whole world is festering,
>   with unhappy souls.
> The French hate the Germans,
>   and the Germans hate the Poles.
> The Italians hate the Yugoslavs.
> The South Africans hate the Dutch,
> And I don't like anybody very much.
> But we can be grateful,
>   and thankful and proud,
> For man is endowed with a mushroom-shaped cloud.
> And we can be certain,
>   that some happy day,
> Someone will set the spark off,
>   And we will all be blown away.
> They're rioting in Africa,

There's strife in Iran,
What nature doesn't do to us,
Will be done by our fellow man.

That song communicated an important fact, something with which we all must deal sometime. *The World is a mess.* We must not only face that fact but we must realize that God has called us to join with Him to try to set the world right. That's why Jesus came into the world. He came because He loves our world and He wants to call together an army of people through whom He can change it back into the wonderful world He willed for it to be when He created it.

When we pray the Lord's Prayer, we are praying for a personal and social revolution through which the transformation of our world will become a reality. There is a plea for a revolution when we pray, 'Thy kingdom come, Thy will be done, on earth as it is in heaven.' Jesus has plans for creating His kingdom right here on earth just as it is in heaven. He wants this world to be the same kind of wonderful place that heaven is. He wants His will to be done, His kingdom to come, right here on this planet and He calls us to join Him in the task of making His will a historical reality. We are the people who have been called by God to join with Him to change the world.

I want to make this as clear as I know how: I want to emphatically assert that Jesus desperately wants you to allow Him to work through you to begin to change His world into the world He wills for it to be.

I know what some of you are thinking, 'Change the world? Me? How could someone like me possibly be used by God to change the world? The world is enormous. It's population is in the billions. It's problems seem unsolvable. It's institutions seem unchangeable. I wouldn't even know how a world revolution could begin.'

Witnessing for Jesus

Well, first of all, the changing of the world begins with people like you and me speaking out and witnessing to what Jesus has done in our personal lives and inviting other people to allow Jesus to change them, too. A lot of people probably don't realize that God's revolution begins with personal evangelism. To change the world, we have to start by changing people. This world is not going to be changed unless the people's hearts and minds and souls are changed. Jesus' plan is to change people and through them to change the world. That's where you come in. You are called to win people to Jesus and to recruit volunteers for His movement. Through the witness of Christians like you and me, He will raise up an array of agents through which He can infiltrate and change every sector and institution of our world.

For ten years I taught at the University of Pennsylvania, one of the top, large American universities. While I was there I taught an advanced seminar. We met weekly for several hours and we talked about all kinds of really heavy stuff. We covered everything from Einstein's theory of relativity to the meaning of life. And one night our discussion got pretty religious. We got to talking about God.

When the lecture was over, some of the guys in the

seminar said, 'Hey! Come back to our apartment. We want to talk to you some more.' So I went back to their apartment and we talked and talked until about two in the morning.

Now, you can't get me talking to people that long without talking about Jesus. Little by little the discussion focused on the Lord. What was neat was that these guys really hadn't heard much about Jesus before. I know some of you are going to have trouble accepting the fact that there really are highly educated people out there who haven't heard much about Jesus. But it's true. There are. As it turned out, a couple of the guys came from Jewish backgrounds. So when I talked to them about Jesus, it was all new stuff to them. They were fascinated. Most of them had never had an in-depth discussion with anyone who had any acquaintance with the New Testament.

We talked and talked and talked. The following week they invited me back to their apartment for another discussion. They invited me again the week after that and the week after that. During the term, one by one, each of the original four guys and the friends they had begun bringing to our Thursday night gatherings became Christians. More than that – they became radically committed Christians. Their zeal for Christ was so intense that they began to have an impact on that campus that you could hardly believe.

One day I was in the bookshop at the university, and one of the leaders of the Hebrew Association came in and looked at me and said, 'Campolo, I don't know whether to bless you or to curse you.' I said, 'Look, if I've got a choice, I'll take the blessing!

What's bothering you?'

He said, 'You know that group of students that gets together on Thursday nights? They never used to come to our meetings before. Now they come every week.' I said, 'That's terrific.' He said, 'That is terrific. Not only do they come, but they're running round the university rounding up all the other Jewish students and bringing them along with them. The place is packed on Friday nights!'

I said, 'You ought to be happy with that.' He said, 'I am. But this is what I don't like. At our meetings we always divide into small groups for discussion and your boys spread themselves out into all of those different discussion groups. And do you know what they're doing in my synagogue?'

Actually, by this point, I didn't have to be told, but I asked anyway. He told me that they were telling the other people in the group about Jesus. 'Campolo, you want to do your evangelizing? Do your evangelizing, I got nothing against it. Just stay out of my synagogue, understand?!'

When I got to the meeting the next Thursday, I said, 'Hey, guys, that was really terrific! I mean, that was pretty amazing! Right up there in the synagogue, you were telling people about Jesus! Man! What a neat way to do it! Where did you come up with that idea?'

One of the guys looked up at me and said, 'From the book of Acts, baby!'

These new Christians witnessed wherever and whenever they could. They knew that part of their mission was to win people to Jesus. They understood better than most church people that Jesus 'saves' us in order that He might use us to reach others with His message and gradually build up a movement through which He can change the world.

When it comes to talking to people about Jesus, nobody can do it better than you. I was the pastor of a church for a while but it wasn't the lifestyle for me. I wish it had been. I would love being the pastor of a church. But being a pastor requires a patience and quality of character that I lack. One of my basic problems was that I never could resist a good one-liner. For instance, one Sunday a lady walking out of the church said to me, 'Reverend, do you know how many grammatical errors you made in the prayer this morning?' Before I could catch myself, I said, 'Lady, I wasn't talking to you anyway.' It wiped her out – but it didn't help my pastoral image.

During the time I was a pastor, I tried to witness for Jesus to people in the community, but it never worked out too well. They always viewed me as 'the clergyman.' Everywhere I went, people's defences went up.

I can remember going to the barber's each week. (This may seem funny to those who know how bald-headed I am.) And every time I walked in, I seemed to interrupt the joking and laughing going on among the other men who were waiting their turns for hair-cuts. As soon as I'd walk in, the barber would say, 'Good morning, *Reverend*' and everybody would freeze. They would quickly slip those semi-porno-graphic magazines under their seats and fold their hands. Then the conversation would always get going slowly. 'Nice weather we're having.' 'Yes, I'm glad it didn't snow. It's too hot to shovel snow,' or something stupid like that.

The only good thing was that they would let me go next in line for my haircut just to get me out of there.

You see, people tend to get all phoney when the clergyman is around. That's why those of you who aren't ministers have an opportunity to witness for Jesus in a way that clergy-types cannot.

Have you heard the story about the little kid who unknowingly comes home during a pastoral call? He doesn't realize that the pastor is there. He just sees his mum and he comes running into this house holding a dead rat by the tail. He says, 'Look, Mum! Look at this rat I caught out behind the barn! I smashed its head in with a baseball bat! I threw rocks at it! I stomped on it! I spit on it and I, I, I . . .' and he looks up and sees the minister, clears his throat and says, 'And, and, and then the dear Lord called it home!'

This ability to change whenever 'the Reverend' shows up is one of the reasons why when it comes to witnessing for Jesus, nobody can do it better than you can. People do not put up the same defences against you as they do against clergy-types. They don't act phoney round you like they do round professional religious people. You may be thinking right about now, 'I don't know whether I can. I don't know whether I have what it takes to really share Jesus with others.' Of course you do. If Jesus has done something in your life, all you have to do is share that with other people. If you love Jesus enough, you'll always find a way to get the story told.

Some time ago, I was invited to be a counsellor at a young people's camp. I don't know how many of you people out there reading this book are Roman Catholics, but that old Roman Catholic theology is right: there is a purgatory. It is young people's camp – a place between heaven and hell where people go to suffer for their sins.

I have never met meaner kids in my life than at this camp. Don't get me wrong. I love young people individually, but the gang at this young people's camp were really bad. Something must happen to young people in a group at camp. They get mean. Let me tell you, *these* young people at *this* camp turned *really* mean. Their meanness was focused on an unfortunate kid named Billy. Billy really broke my heart because he had been born with a whole host of birth defects. He had cerebral palsy and his brain was unable to exercise proper control over the movements of his body or his speech. The other kids mocked him. They called him 'spastic.' Billy would walk across the grounds of the camp in his disjointed manner, and the others would line up behind him, imitating him and mimicking his every movement. They thought that this was funny. It was the worst kind of young people's cruelty I had ever seen.

One day I watched as Billy asked one of the boys a question, 'Which way is the craft shop?' The other boy twisted up grotesquely, pointed a dozen different ways and said, 'That way!' I felt like punching out that mean kid. How could he be so cruel to a handicapped boy?

The level of meanness reached its lowest point on a Wednesday morning. Billy's dormitory had been assigned the morning devotions for that camp of 150 kids. All of the boys in his dormitory had voted for

46

Billy to be the speaker. I knew, and they knew, that he couldn't do it; they just wanted to get him up there so that they could mock him and laugh. They thought it would be fun to watch 'spastic Billy' try to deliver a devotional talk. I was irate. And I was livid. I was seething with anger as little Billy got up out of his seat and limped his way to the platform. You could hear the titters of mocking laughter and sneering going through the group. I could not remember ever being so angry. What was amazing was that the ridicule of the boys didn't stop that boy. He took his place behind the rostrum and started to speak. It took Billy almost ten tortured minutes to say, 'Je-sus loves meee! Je-Je-Je-sus loves meee! Annd-I-I-love Je-Je-Jesus.' And when he finished there was dead silence. I looked over my shoulder, and there were boys shaking and trembling and crying all over the place.

A revival broke out in that camp and young people turned their lives over to Jesus. A host of boys committed their lives to Christian service. I wish I had kept count of how many ministers I have met as I travel across the USA who have told me that they gave their lives to Jesus because of the witness of a 'spastic' kid named Billy.

If God could use him with all of his limitations, what makes you think that God can't use you to touch the lives of other people? If God can transform the lives of people through the likes of little Billy, don't you dare tell me He can't do great things through you.

A revolution of change...for Jesus

I hope I have made it clear that when we talk about God's revolution, our first responsibility is to witness for Christ. God's revolution begins with people like you and me winning others to this movement called Christianity. God's revolution is dependent upon having a host of agents who can be deployed in every sector of society. Then these revolutionaries not only can share the message of Jesus but can begin to bring about the kinds of changes that God wills for society. Change agents for God's revolution are needed in every social institution and business. They are needed in every school, every university, every office, every trades union, every television studio, every farm, every county council – and most important – in every family. Many people underrate the importance of what goes on in the home, but I am convinced that of all the social institutions that must be brought under the lordship of Christ, none takes precedence over the family.

A case in point: my wife is a really appealing person, the most articulate person I know. She can really talk; she has a way with words that staggers my imagination. And I love it whenever we're at some social gathering and somebody, like some woman lawyer, comes and says, in her most condescending voice, 'And what is it that you do, my dear?' Most of you reading this book probably aren't married, so you might not realize that such a question is often a disguised put-down of homemakers by those who think that the only significant work in society is in some professional vocation.

48

My wife has the greatest comeback in the world, something you can use when you get married. When somebody asks, 'And what is that you do, my dear?' she answers, 'I am socializing two Homo sapiens into the dominant values of the Judeo-Christian tradition in order that they might be instruments for the transformation of the social order into the kinds of eschatological utopia that God willed from the beginning of creation.' Then she usually looks back at the other person and asks, 'And what is it that you do?' Often, the reply, 'I'm a lawyer' is made in a very subdued voice.

I don't know what your job will be, whether you will be a lawyer, a musician, a labourer, an artist, a business person or a government worker. But if you are a committed Christian, that is, if you are committed to the revolution which God is carrying out in our world, you should be asking, 'How can I change things where I work so that things will be set up more in accord with the will of God? How can I restructure the organization of my workplace so that the principles of God's justice are put into action?' Those of you who will be housewives or househusbands ought to be asking the same kinds of questions. You should be asking, 'How can I change things in the house so that my family functions more in accord with the will of God? How can I promote the kind of family life that will express the revolutionary principles which Jesus outlined for us in the Scriptures?'

When I used the word 'househusband,' I did so for a reason. Being a *househusband* is becoming a real possibility these days. It's happening everywhere. In many families wives are securing jobs outside the house and husbands are opting to become home-makers. I can just read the thoughts of some of the guys who are reading this book. *Househusband?!* Wouldn't that be terrific? Play tennis all morning, watch the soap operas all afternoon!

If that's what you think, you men just don't know what keeping house is really like. It's a jungle in there. You'll work harder keeping house with a couple of kids under your feet than you would ever have to work in any factory or office. You should try doing housework sometime. What's worse is that there are a thousand and one put-downs to be endured in that job. For instance, it's hard enough to keep house without having television ads constantly reminding you of ways in which you might be failing. Try the ad in which a housewife is reduced to tears by a whining voice chanting, 'Ring around the collar, ring around the collar!' She's being condemned because her detergent didn't get rid of the dirt inside the collar of her husband's shirt. The ad never asks the right question, *'Why doesn't he wash his neck?'*

In the home, in the market-place, in schools, in government – everywhere – God needs people who will implement the principles of His revolution and work to change the world. Ask yourself, 'What needs to change at the place where I live and work if God is to be pleased?' Then commit yourself to effect that change.

I had a friend who understood that being a Christian was not only telling others about Jesus, but changing the way things happened at the job. He understood that his work style was to express his commitment to God's revolution. He realized that he was supposed to implement in his vocational activities the principles of the kingdom of God and thus undermine the present social order with the new order which is in accord with God's Word.

This friend and I were at college together. He went on to teach at Trenton State University and I went to teach at Eastern College. After teaching at Trenton State for about three weeks, he walked into the dean's office and said, 'I'm not coming back tomorrow. I'm quitting this job. I thought you should know.'

The dean said, 'You can't walk out on a teaching position in the middle of term.'

My friend responded, 'Watch me!'

Later his mother telephoned me and said, 'Tony, you have to go and talk to Charlie. He quit his job. He's a Ph.D. in English literature and if he doesn't teach, what can he possibly do?' Now, I have to admit, that *is* a good question. What *do* you do with a Ph.D. in English if you don't teach?

So I hunted him out. I found him living in an attic flat in Hamilton Square, New Jersey. I've got to admit I liked the flat. He had travel posters on his walls, shelves and shelves of books, a stereo; he had the whole 'with it' scene. As I walked into the flat, he said, 'Sit down, man. Sit down.' So I sat down – in one of those bean-bag chairs. Did you ever sit in one of those things? It was like a giant amoeba. That chair threatened to devour me right on the spot.

As I sat down there in that chair, half-consumed and half-digested, he looked at me with a Buddha-like smile and said, 'I quit, Tony. I quit.'

I said, 'I know you quit, Charlie. Why did you quit?'

He said, 'I can't teach man. I can't teach those people. Every time I walked into that class and gave a lecture, I died a little.'

Now I can understand that. I'm a teacher. I know what it is like to go into a class and share truth. Truth! Real truth! Truth wrenched from existential suffering! Truth gleaned from the pains of human existence! And after I have shared Truth with my students, after I've let every nerve and sinew tingle with the excitement of grappling with ultimate truth, some kid on the last row raises his hand and asks, 'Do we have to know this for the final?' And I die a little bit.

So I empathized with Charlie. I understood him. And it wasn't long before I realized that I couldn't dissuade him from his decision to give up teaching. Finally, I said, 'What are you doing now? How are you feeding yourself?'

He said, 'I'm a postman.'

I said, 'That's terrific. A Ph.D. postman.'

He shot back. 'There aren't too many of us!'

I couldn't change his mind, so I came back with the old Protestant work ethic thing. I said, 'Charlie, if you're gonna be a postman, be the *best* postman you can be.'

He looked at me with a silly grin and said, 'I'm a lousy postman.'

I asked, 'What do you mean, you're a lousy postman?'

He answered, 'Everybody else gets the post delivered by one o'clock, but I never get back until about five-thirty or six.'

'What takes you so long?' I wanted to know.

He said, 'I visit! That's why it takes so long. You wouldn't believe how many people on my round never got visited until I became the postman. But I've got this problem, I can't sleep at nights.'

I asked, 'Why can't you sleep?'

He said, 'Who can sleep after drinking twenty cups of coffee?'

I began to get the image of this postman on the job. He was no ordinary postman. I could picture him going from door to door and at each home giving more than the post. I could see him visiting solitary widows, counselling troubled teenagers, joking with lonely old men. I could see him delivering the post in a way that was revolutionary for the people on his round.

He's the only postman I know that on his birthday, the people on his round get together, hire a gym and throw a party for him. They love him because he's a postman who expresses the love of Jesus everywhere he goes. In his own subtle way, my friend Charlie is changing his world, changing the lives of people, touching them where they are, making a difference in their lives. It may not sound like much, but that man who is delivering the post as Jesus would deliver the post is an agent of God who is changing the world.

Just as a homemaker doing the job as Jesus would want it done becomes a person through whom God can change things in this world; just as a postman delivering post like Jesus would deliver it is a revolutionary, so can you as students begin to bring about the new world which God wills by the ways in which you function at your schools, colleges or universities. Young people, do you realize what your opportunity is? You have a chance to go into your school or college and share Jesus Christ. Not just in words, but in the way you treat people. You can be an agent through which God can begin to change your school or college into the sort of place he wants it to be.

Although all British schools are meant to have a daily act of worship, in practice most schools adopt a neutral position, and the responsibility to witness is put right where it ought to be – on the students in schools.

So wherever you are studying you are the ones who must carry Jesus into your classrooms. You must be God's agents. You must reveal Christ to the people at school. You can do it by the way you conduct yourselves, by the way in which you treat other people, and in how you talk to your teachers. You help to further God's revolution by the ways in which you change things at your school. You are the agents of God's revolution at your school.

We witness by what we say, but we also witness and exercise an influence for change by what we do. It's part of the whole theme of being an instrument of God in the world.

As a sociologist I will never underestimate the importance of the 'foolishness of preaching,' as the Scripture says – converting people to Jesus. I know how working for change in the places where you are employed, go to school and live, can influence society. However, I also know that we must do more than these things if we are to change the world. Furthermore, the Bible declares that we are called to do more than tell people about Jesus and exercise an influence for the kingdom of God.

Changing the world

For those of you who are willing to get a little intellectual, let me tell you what a Dutch theologian named Hendrick Berkhof has to teach us from the Scriptures. Berkhof wrote a whole book explaining a phrase that is used over and over by the apostle Paul, 'principalities and powers.' If you know the New Testament, you know that phrase. We read in Ephesians 6:12, 'Brothers and sisters, we wrestle not only against flesh and blood, but against principalities and powers and the rulers of the age.'

That verse tells us that in the process of living the Christian life we must struggle against Satan on two levels. First of all, we must fight against what Satan is trying to do to us through 'the flesh.' You guys reading this know what this is all about, right? I don't know about girls, I can only write from a male perspective and speak from experience. But I do know about the guys. I do know that guys have great problems overcoming what Satan is trying to do to them through the flesh.

The truth of the matter is that we all have flesh problems. Sigmund Freud understood this when he said that there are sexual urges that overpower our psyches. Freud discovered that the sexual powers in the normal person are so awesome that nothing – not even cultural restraints – can defuse or negate them.

Of course, Sigmund Freud didn't know what Jesus could do. He did not know that Christ can enable an individual to control his or her sexual drives and direct them into constructive and humanizing love relationships. Freud did not know that with Jesus an individual is able to overcome the destructive tendencies of sexuality. If I know anything about the teenage years, it is this – without the help of Jesus, sex can destroy you.

You have all seen kids in your school who have messed up their lives because of sex. It really can ruin your life, your dreams and your future. I don't have to paint you pictures to let you know what can happen when sexual drives get out of control.

We all must struggle against the sexual tendencies inherent in the flesh, but the good news is that Jesus joins us in this struggle and helps us to overcome the demonic designs for our sex lives. When our flesh is weak, when we find that we cannot overcome sexual temptation, then we know that we can invite Him to work through us and strengthen us. We can ask Him to make us conquerors over the flesh.

I don't know about the rest of you guys, but I know in my own life that I get turned on easily. Some of you are thinking, 'Doc, you're supposed to be a spiritual guy. You're not supposed to get turned on.' Well, I do. I get turned on for a very simple reason. I'm human. So was Jesus. And what's more, Jesus got turned on. You say, 'Not Jesus! That's sacriligious!'

But remember the Bible says that He was tempted in all ways as we are tempted, but He had within Himself the power of the Father. Because He depended on the strength of His Father He was able to overcome all and any temptations and remain 'without sin.' That same power is available to us, so when in fact you and I do succumb to the lust of the flesh, we can never say, 'Oh well, I'm only human.' God meant for you to be more than human; in your humanness He meant for you to depend upon His power to overcome the lusts of the flesh.

Not only does He want us to overcome the flesh, but Ephesians 6:12 tells us that He also wants us to overcome the *'principalities and powers.'* Hendrick Berkhof tries to explain to us what the apostle Paul means when he uses that phrase: 'Principalities and powers' are the societal forces and institutional structures that influence us and constrain our behaviour. They include the social institutions to which we belong and which have so much to do with what we are and how we act. 'Principalities and powers' are all of those elements of the culture in which we live that condition what we do. Are we *really* influenced by the 'principalities and powers' you ask?

You bet we are. For instance, television is one of the 'principalities and powers,' and no one would question the fact that television moulds us. Films are 'principalities and powers,' and they mould us, too. As a matter of fact, I would say that most of you reading this book are moulded by the media far more than you are moulded by the Holy Spirit. That's something we have to change. We must stop being controlled by the media. We must struggle to allow ourselves more and more to come under the control of the Holy Spirit. It's easy to see that we are media creations by the way we dress, the way we talk, the way we act – almost everything we do is influenced by the media. The apostle Paul tells us that we must struggle against the influence of this 'principality and power.'

Does the educational system mould us? Of course it does. Does the political system mould us? Of course it does. Do large industries mould our behaviour? Of course they do. The Bible teaches us, particularly in Paul's epistle to the Colossians, that Satan is able to use the 'principalities and powers' to influence us to do things that are contrary to the will of God. As Christians we are called upon not to conform to what the demonically controlled 'principalities and powers' condition us to do. The Bible says in Romans 12:2, 'Be not conformed to this world but be ye transformed by the renewing of your mind, that ye may prove what is that good, and acceptable, and perfect, will of God.'

However, as Christian revolutionaries, we are called not only to resist the influences of the 'principalities and powers' but to take them over and bring them under the Lordship of Christ. Or, to put it more simply, we are commissioned by God to change each and every social institution of our society so that they all function as God wants them to function and influence people in the way God wants them influenced. Let me tell you about one attempt by some Christians to do just that.

A group of my students became very, very upset with one large multinational corporation, Gulf and Western Industries. While we were doing some missionary work in the Dominican Republic, we became aware of the fact that this huge multinational corporation was taking land that should have been used to grow food for needy people in that poor country – and using that land to grow sugar.

As you probably know, sugar is bad for you to begin with. So is coffee. So is tobacco. You should know that if all of the land in the world that is presently being used to grow sugar, coffee and tobacco – all of which poison our systems – were used to grow food, we could cut malnutrition in the Third World by almost 50 per cent.

Anyway, we were upset with Gulf and Western because we saw that they were growing sugar for people in the United States on land that we felt should have been used to grow food for needy Dominican peasants.

I think you'll find our method of protest interesting. There were eleven of us, and each of us bought one share of stock in the company. I don't know how many millions of shares of stock there are in Gulf and Western, but we owned eleven of them. It is important for you to realize that you only need one share to go to the annual stockholders' meeting. So each of us 'stockholders' went to the meeting and we said our piece.

We were probably somewhat arrogant about it, but we really laid into them! 'Hey! We don't like the way you are running this company! This company belongs to God.' In private confrontations following that meeting, we met with some of the company's top executives and we told them the Bible story of a certain man who had a vineyard. The man went away on a long journey, but the people he left in charge of the vineyard didn't run it right. He sent messengers, but they wouldn't listen to the messengers. Then he sent his son, but the people put him to death. Jesus ends that parable with this question, 'What then should the owner of the vineyard do to the unfaithful stewards when he returns?'

We told all of that and more to those guys. 'This

company belongs, in the end, to God. You are His stewards. He doesn't like the way you are running the company, so we have come as messengers. You had better listen to us, or God is going to come and get you.'

Now that was sheer arrogance. Looking back on our behaviour I have to admit we weren't at all Christlike or *even fair*. But what followed those encounters was incredible. We found out that the leaders of that company weren't bad men. It took us a while to come to grips with that. But little by little we became convinced that they were good and decent men. The more we talked, the more we interacted and the more we became aware that they wanted to do what was right. In our talks with them they convinced us that they wanted Gulf and Western to be an instrument for good in the Dominican Republic.

About a year and a half after our discussions with Gulf and Western began, I got a phone call from one of the executives of that corporation. He said, 'Tomorrow we're going to have a press conference and part of the reason we're holding the press conference is to make an accouncement about some of the issues we discussed with you. We want you to be among the first to know what's going to happen.'

And as I sat there dumbfounded, that executive told me they were going to announce that Gulf and Western was going to do the following: they would test the soil that made up their land holdings in the Dominican Republic and determine what land could be used to grow food. That land would then be shifted from the production of sugar to the production of food. Secondly, the company would make a commitment to build forty thousand new housing units for the sugar workers so that they would no longer have to live in the slums. Thirdly, Gulf and Western would provide educational and health programmes, particularly in the eastern half of the country where their operations were located. The spokesman went on to say that his corporation had made a commitment of 100 million dollars to be spent over the following five years in order to make all the promises a reality. Now that's incredible!

Don't tell me corporations can't change. Don't tell me the system is evil and beyond redemption. I think that if we go to corporate executives, hopefully without arrogance, and with reasonable expectations of what needs to be changed and why, calling upon them to respond to the things that the Bible teaches, their responses might exceed our expectations.

The problem with us is that we all know what to say to drunks, alcoholics, drug addicts and criminals. They are beneath us. But we don't know how to talk to the leaders of the 'principalities and powers.' We don't have the guts to challenge those who hold positions of power to try to change the political and economic structures of our society in order that they might function more in accord with the will of God. Jesus calls us to be agents of change, to participate with Him in changing the world into the kind of world He wants it to be.

I want you to become a revolutionary for Jesus. When I ask you to be a revolutionary, I don't mean that I want you to get a gun and do something violent. I'm asking you to do something else. I'm asking you to seriously consider – right this very minute – going to some Third World country to do something for Jesus among people who have real needs. Some of you should consider being servants of God to the poor. All of you should give serious consideration to the possibility of becoming missionaries. I don't know if you realize that God not only wants to make your own country better; He wants to transform people and 'principalities and powers' in every nation of the world. He wants His revolutionaries at work everywhere.

Setting a course and travelling light

So today's young person must ask not only, 'What can I do to best serve Jesus?' He or she must also ask, 'Where can I go?' This is something you should be thinking about now.

When I was growing up, a missionary speaker would sometimes say to our youth group, 'Some of you ought to consider going to the mission field and the rest will stay at home and support you.' In this day and age, I think the reverse should be said. We should tell a typical youth group, 'Most of you ought to consider going, and the only people who ought to stay here at home are the people who are really called to do so.' I mean, if God is calling you to be a schoolteacher in a cosy suburb, you ought to be one. As I said earlier, every school is in need of the transforming presence of Christian revolutionaries. If He is calling you to be a lawyer, do it. God needs revolutionaries in the legal profession.

But it seems to me that unless you have a specific call to serve God here in your own home country, you have a responsibility to consider going to that place in the world where you are most needed. And where are you most needed today? There's a likelihood that it won't be in your good old safe home country. Why should anybody want to be a schoolteacher in some place like suburban Houston or suburban London when he or she could be a schoolteacher in Haiti?

You could be a teacher in a Third World school where children would run and jump all over you, hug you and kiss you because you were there. You don't see many teachers around here getting hugged and kissed, do you? Why would you want to be a doctor in your cosy home country, when you could be in some village in Africa where you would be urgently needed, where you could be an answer to a desperate need?

Each of us has a responsibility to be in the places where we are most needed. Each of us is called to do something heroic for Jesus. You could be a translator of the Scriptures. Imagine going into a tribe that has never had the Bible, learning the language, translating the Bible into that language, teaching the people to read that language, and sharing Jesus with them. From that day on for the rest of their lives, for the rest of their history, whenever members of that tribe quoted John 3:16, it would be because *you* went there and made it possible.

Wouldn't you like to do something fantastic like that with your life? God needs not one, not ten, not a thousand, but He needs a hundred thousand young people to rise up and go to places where they are desperately needed in the next five years.

After most people graduate from college or university, they say to themselves, 'What am I going to do with myself?' I wish I could tell each of them, *'Do something great for Jesus.'*

One last but very important thing: if you are going to be a revolutionary for Jesus, you've got to change your personal lifestyle.

One day back in the counter-culture years of the 1960s I was lecturing to my 'Introduction to Sociology' class (which numbered several hundred students) when in the middle of the lecture a 'way out' looking student stood up and shouted, 'Bull! Bull! Bull! Bull!'

I yelled, 'Sit down, fella! Sit down or you're in serious trouble!'

He shouted back, *'Who cares?'*

I said, 'Fella, if you don't sit down I'm going to throw you out of this class.'

He yelled back, *'Who cares?'*

I said, 'You don't seem to understand. If I throw you out of class, you're not getting back in.'

He yelled, *'Who cares?'*

I didn't push it. I'm sure that if I had said, 'You get thrown out of this class, you're going to be tossed out of this university,' he would have yelled, *'Who cares?'* And if I had told him that if he got thrown out of the university, he wouldn't be able to get a job, he would have yelled, *'Who cares?'* And if I had said that without a job he wouldn't have money to buy all the stuff that America says he ought to have, he would have yelled back at me, *Who cares?'*

You can't really be a revolutionary agent for Jesus, unless you can look at this world and what it's trying to sell you and yell at the top of your lungs, *'Who cares?'*

Do you really care about the things of this world more than you care about serving Jesus? Let me tell you that as long as you must have what this society has to offer, this society will control you.

I control my students because they want good grades. I can give them good grades; therefore I have control over them. I can make them read books they don't want to read and write papers they don't want to write. I can even make them stay up all night studying for tests they don't want to take. That's my power. And do you know why I have that power? Because they want what I can give them.

Our Western society will control you and you will be its slave until you can say to this society and everything that it has to offer, *'Who cares!'* The cars, the houses, the whole shooting match. If you've got them, enjoy them – but if you're going to be a revolutionary for Jesus you must be the kind of person who can do without any of these things.

I was at a convention of some Mennonite people a while ago. Mennonites, as you may know, are supposed to be pacifists. However, at this convention, an older man made a statement suggesting that perhaps the Mennonites ought to become more like the rest of the people in the world and give up their historical pacifist stance. A young man stood to challenge him.

I can still remember the older man looking back at him sternly and saying, 'It's all right for you to talk that way, but one of these days, the Russians will come and take everything you've got.'

The young man smiled and said, 'If they come, they really can't take everything I've got. You see, when I became a Christian I gave everything I had to

65

Jesus. So if the Russians come and take that stuff, they'll be taking what belongs to Him and that's His problem.'

The older man responded, 'All right, but don't forget that they can kill you.' The young man came back, sharp as a tack, and said, 'They can't kill me. You see, mister, I'm already dead.'

(The guy was right, that's what the Bible means when it tells us that Christians are 'people who have died.' When you become a Christian, who you were dies and a new self is born. And the new self that is born can never die.)

The older man looked back at that young man and said, 'All right, maybe they can't kill you and maybe they can't take what you have, but they can make you suffer.'

Then the young man smiled and said, 'When that day comes, I hope I have the grace to repeat the Bible verse, "Blessed are ye when men shall revile you and persecute you and say all manner of evil against you falsely for My sake. Rejoice and be exceedingly glad, for so persecuted they the prophets which were before you."'

The young man turned to the rest of us and said, 'That's the secret of freedom. If you don't have anything, if you're already dead, and if you rejoice when people torture you, then there isn't much they can do to you. There just isn't any way they can threaten you, is there?'

The time may come when we will have to stand up and be counted for Jesus. The question I have to ask you is this: 'Do you love Jesus enough to be able to say to this world, and all it has to offer, "Who cares?"'

Will you be as free to follow Jesus as the young man I've just described? Will you be the kind of revolutionary who has committed everything he or she is and has to the cause? If your answer to these questions is 'Yes,' your lifestyle will radically change. You will have a different value system governing your thinking, a different criteria affecting your decisions, and a different set of concerns controlling your spending habits.

Take Christmas, for instance. At Christmas your biggest problem is what to buy for somebody who already has everything. From a radically Christian perspective, you know what to buy for somebody who has everything? Nothing! It would be wild if your parents came down the stairs, looked at all of the kids sitting next to the Christmas tree, and said, 'Nobody's getting anything for Christmas this year because everybody's already got everything.'

Now that would be the right thing to do, wouldn't it? What right do we have to buy surplus junk at Christmas time, when there are kids who are starving and suffering from malnutrition all over the world? What do you think?

I'm going to lay it on you heavy: say you've got £200 and you want to buy a stereo. On the other hand, you know that the £200 can feed fifty kids in Bangladesh. You can do one of two things. You can buy the stereo, or you can buy food for the hungry kids. Which of the two do you think Jesus would do? Would He buy the stereo, or would He feed the hungry kids? You *know* He'd feed the hungry kids every time. Isn't a Christian someone who tries to do what Jesus would do?

The question each of us must ask is why do we continue to spend our money on (as the Scripture says) 'things that satisfy you not'?

The time has come for a whole new generation of young people to come along; a generation of young people who do not live for themselves; a generation of young people who want to do something for Jesus; a generation of young people who want to do something for others; a generation of young people who want to do something heroic with their lives.

A couple of years ago I took my son and daughter to Haiti where some of us from Eastern College have helped to develop a school and orphanage. A lot of the money that I could have spent on my two children has been sent down to Haiti to be spent on the building of this little school, which now has fifty students in it. My children had never been to the school before. After arriving in Port-au-Prince, we got into the jeep and drove out to visit the place. After about twenty miles, the road was no longer made up. But we kept travelling. We crossed some fields and eventually came to a clump of trees, on the other side of which was the school. We drove round the trees and there it was. It was the twenty-eighth of December and school was not in session, but I knew what we would find. All fifty kids were there waiting to greet us.

When they saw us, the kids let out a scream! My two children got out of the jeep and those fifty kids jumped all over them, grabbed them, hugged them and kissed them. Then they lined up and sang a song that they had learned in English just for us: 'Jesus loves the little children, all the children of the world, red and yellow, black and white, they are precious in His sight.'

Each of the children took a turn reciting Bible verses for us. Some of them had made us gifts. They were Christmas tree ornaments made of sticks and string: not much to look at, but somehow very precious.

We gathered up the presents from those grateful children, got into the jeep and headed back to the capital city. My boy and girl, who are usually very, very talkative, seemed unusually quiet during the return trip. About half-way back to Port-au-Prince, I looked at my son, who seemed rather pensive, and asked him what he was thinking. He said to me, 'Dad, there isn't anything you could have done with that money that would have made me happier than I am right now.'

Believe me, there is nothing you can do with your life that will make you happier than giving it away to others for Jesus. There is nothing that generates more thrills than using whatever you have in accord with the will of God. When you say, 'Jesus, use what I have and am for your cause and the sake of others,' you will discover unparalleled gratification. When you can honestly say, 'Lord, begin to change the world through me,' you will discover how fulfilling life can be.

I know we're not going to perfect this world; that won't happen until the second coming occurs. At the end of history Jesus is coming back to this world and on that day *He* will make the world perfect. However, I believe that God wants to initiate through us a movement that will begin to make the changes which

He will complete when He returns. He wants to start His great revolution now – and with you. He wants to know if you will allow Him to use you to begin to change the world. You can go into government, you can go into our economic structures, you can go into our educational systems, or you can go into the emerging Third World countries and become instruments for changing the world. You can use your talents and your financial resources for the cause of Christ. You can know the excitement of participating in God's revolution.

In *The Waste Land*, T. S. Eliot writes: 'This is the way the world will end, this is the way the world will end, this is the way the world will end, Not with a bang, but a whimper.'

He was wrong. This world is not going to end with a bang and it's not going to end with a whimper. The good news about the way the world will end is that the kingdoms of this world will become the kingdom of our God, and He shall reign for ever and ever. Hallelujah!

The truth of the matter is that we are on the verge of conquering the world for Jesus, and I'm inviting you to become witnesses, to become persons who influence people everywhere you go to join God's revolution. I'm inviting you to allow Jesus to make you into somebody who will go into every corner of the world, especially to those places where you are most desperately needed. I am calling you to go where you will make a world of difference in a world that yearns to be different. I'm asking you to let Jesus use you to begin to change His world.

You've probably heard this line a dozen times

before. Most of you have grown up hearing this stuff. But you haven't done anything about it. You haven't acted.

Soren Kierkegaard tells about a make-believe country where only ducks live. On Sunday morning all the ducks came into church, waddled down the aisle, waddled into their pews, and squatted. Then the duck minister came in, took his place behind the pulpit, opened the Duck Bible and read, 'Ducks! You have wings, and with wings, you can fly like eagles. You can soar into the sky! Ducks! You have wings!' All the ducks yelled 'Amen!' and then they all waddled home.

Maybe you have heard everything I've said before, but you have never acted on it. Maybe you've understood the radical nature of the call to discipleship but you have never done anything about it. Maybe you've known for a long time that being a Christian means joining God's revolution, but you've never been willing to make a commitment to His cause. You, like the ducks in Kierkegaard's story, have not acted on the message you have heard. Well, the time has come to act – to do – to join – to commit.

Jesus is here right now, and He is saying to you, 'Give Me your life. Join My revolution. Participate in My great movement in history. For My sake, in response to what I've done for you – give Me your life to do My will.'

A friend of mine was on a train travelling out of Victoria Station in London. Across from him in the compartment were two men in their early thirties. Twenty minutes out of the station, one of them had an epileptic seizure. Perhaps you know how frigh-

71

YOU CAN MAKE A DIFFERENCE

tening such a seizure can be. The man stiffened and
fell heavily out of his seat. Immediately, his friend
took off his own jacket, rolled it up and put it behind
his friend's head. He blotted the beads of perspiration
from his brow with his handkerchief, talked to the
stricken man in a quiet manner and calmed him.
When the seizure was over, he lifted his friend gently
back into his seat.

Then he turned to my friend and said, 'Mister,
please forgive us. Sometimes this happens two or
three times a day. My buddy and I were in Vietnam
together, and we were both wounded. I had bullets in
both my legs and he had one in his shoulder. The
helicopter that was supposed to come for us never
came to pick us up.

'My friend picked me up, mister, and he carried
me for three and a half days out of that jungle. The
Viet Cong were sniping at us the whole way. He was
in more agony than I was. I begged him to drop me
and save himself, but he wouldn't let me go. He got
me out of that jungle, mister. He saved my life. I
don't know how he did it and I don't know why he
did it.

'Four years ago, I found out that he had this
condition, so I sold my house in New York, took what
money I had, and came over here to take care of him.'
And then he looked at his friend and said, 'You see,
mister, after what he did for me, *there isn't anything I
wouldn't do for him.*'

I'm not going to give the big fanfare or drum roll
here. There's no choir singing 'Just as I Am.' Nevertheless, I want to ask you something while you are
reading these words. I ask you to say, 'I want to

commit my life to Christian service. I'm ready to become a revolutionary for Jesus. I am not just going to believe in Jesus; I am going to surrender to Him without any reservations. God can use me to do anything He wants, anywhere He wants. I'll go wherever and say whatever and do whatever He leads. I am His without reservation, and if this means the mission field, I'm ready to go.'

Sometimes when I raise this challenge at youth rallies, I see dozens of hands raised high. And I say, 'My God, are you serious? I mean, are you *really* serious? Are there really this many kids ready to say, I'm ready to go anywhere, do anything'? If all of you are serious, the revolution is about to explode!'

DATING
Turning Your Love Life over to Jesus

3

Boyfriends and girlfriends...
and Jesus

Let's talk about young people's favourite topic, dating. Not simply because this is something that every kid wants to discuss and think about, but because this will exercise a decisive influence on how you carry out your Christian commitment. You know and I know that there are few things more important to young people between the ages of 16 and 24 than who you go out with. If you are going to be a Christian, it is important that you behave right on dates. It is important that you marry right. You mess up this area of your life, and you are likely to mess up your Christian commitment. I know of more kids who had fantastic promise for Christian service who blew it because they didn't date right.

I started going out with girls in my final year at secondary school. That was a little late compared to other guys my age. And as I started dating, I was amazed to discover how much it cost. Dating is wildly expensive. I took this one girl out four times and I spent a total of $24.32 on her. Girls always laugh and say 'cheapskate' when I admit that I was keeping track of how much I spent. But you guys know what I'm talking about. Of course guys keep track, because money spent on a girl while you're going out with her is an investment. If you spend a lot of money on them, they are obligated to you, right?

Now, girls, if you don't like the idea that you become obligated when a guy spends a lot of money on you, then perhaps you ought to take a note or two from the pages of the feminist handbook and not let him spend that much money on you. If you don't want to be manipulated into a stage of obligation to a guy, you should consider 'going Dutch.'

One day I came into the lunchroom at West Philadelphia High, and there was my girl – my $24.32 girl – sitting there talking to another guy. And she wasn't just small-talking, she was serious-talking. I went over to the guy sitting next to her and said, 'You ought to leave, see.' In today's language, I would say something like, 'Get lost.' The guy disappeared in a hurry.

My girl looked at me with a steel-like look and said, 'Tony, I've been out with you four times and you act like you own me.' I said, 'Agnes (I can't help it, that was her name!), for $24.32, I bought you!'

I know that was a terrible thing to say, but I really felt I had a claim on her. The girls reading this book probably are saying to themselves, 'You know, that's what's the matter with guys. They go out with you a few times and spend a few bucks on you and they act like they own you.'

This is just one of the things that is wrong with our dating system. Dating is too expensive and because of the expense, guys tend to want to go steady. I wanted to go steady as soon as I started dating because I, like you, know the following to be true: you spend the most money on a girl during the early stages of dating. Once you go steady, it's different. When kids go steady they mostly hang around the house (usually the girl's house) and drink Cokes (usually bought by her parents). And when things get boring, they neck.

The cost leads people to be manipulated into going steady and it definitely leaves the girls with a sense of being obligated to the guys. This often results in girls doing things with guys that they really would rather not do. At the very least, an expensive evening out requires an obligatory goodnight kiss from the girl.

I worry about the Christian implications of this way of doing things. Does the Lord really want you to allow yourself to be manoeuvred into a position where you have to deliver certain signs of affection that you neither mean nor intend?

But there is another thing wrong with the dating system which from a Christian perspective is far more serious, and that is the value system that is implied in it. The system tends to get young people to put a premium on personal traits and characteristics which, in the long range of life, prove to be superficial. On the contrary, a number of things that really count in personal relationships are ignored. The young people who make it in the dating system are usually good-looking, but may be shallow, while many quality people who aren't so good-looking don't stand a chance.

Those who are hurting

I never really saw the horror of all of this until my final year at West Philadelphia High when I was elected student government president. That was a real ego trip. Being president of a student body of 4,500 students had me feeling like somebody special.

Then I realized that one of the things which went with the job was this: I was responsible for setting up and running the dances the school had each month. The trouble was that I belonged to one of those churches that didn't approve of dancing. Many a time our preacher would pound his pulpit and tell us, 'Dancing stimulates the lust of the flesh!' Every time he laid that on us, I would start to fantasize and mumble to myself, 'Yeah!' Of course I have to say that he was probably right. If a couple of teenagers can gyrate face to face for three hours and not get turned on, they are not spiritual – they are dead! I think there is a naiveté about our thinking if we think that it is possible to dance suggestively without getting turned on. When kids get into that kind of dancing too heavily, they should not be surprised if their erotic feelings get out of hand.

Of course fundamental churches like the one I went to back then can often be hypocritical. My church did not approve of dancing (because it stimulated the lust of the flesh), but our church did have 'hayrides' – outings with a hay wagon. Here there was always some guy with a guitar in the front of the wagon playing 'Do Lord' while everybody else was in the straw 'doing it.' It's amazing to see how we evangelical Christians can be so blind to the consequences of what we do, while we self-righteously knock what others do.

Since our church didn't have dances and I was against dances, I told my high school principal how I felt. He said, 'You've got to do it, Tony. It is one of the responsibilities of the student body president.' I finally gave in and on the appointed night did my job and got ready for the dance. I had decided I would go but would not dance. I would be what sociologists call an 'observer participant.' I would appear to be a participant in the dance, but really would not get involved. So that night I was with the other kids and yet I was an outsider, observing what was going on with a clarity that somebody who was actually dancing could not have. What I saw was incredible.

Along with the decorating committee, I got to school about 6.30 to set up for the dance. We got the old crêpe paper out and strung it diagonally across the gym. We set up folding chairs against the walls. Then we opened the windows of the gym because the basketball team had just finished practising, and nobody likes to dance in the smell of a giant armpit!

After we had aired out the place, at about a quarter to seven, this kid named Roger (that's not his real name) showed up. Frankly, Roger was a loser. I mean, this kid was a disaster on wheels. I wondered, as he walked in, 'Why has Roger come? Nobody is going to want to dance with him. Most of the girls don't even like talking to him. Why is he here?'

But Roger had not come to dance. He had brought a stack of records and he was counting on being the disc jockey. He went up on the platform in the back of the gym where there was a record player and he played the records while the other kids danced. He played disc jockey all night. This was Roger's way of participating without getting hurt. He knew that if he ever stopped playing the records, came down from

81

the platform and asked some girl to dance, he would probably be rejected. Playing records was Roger's way of being involved in the dance without getting hurt.

I still remember the teacher who was chaperoning the dance coming up to me at the interval and saying, 'Hey, Tony, this is a wonderful dance! Everybody is having such a good time.' And I looked at Roger and I wondered whether he was having a good time. I think not. I think Roger was hurting, hurting bad.

He wasn't the only one, either. Sitting round the gym on the folding chairs were about forty girls, all sitting there with bored looks of indifference on their faces. You know the looks, looks that say, 'Oh, wow, this is a real drag; when is it going to end?' But you know what those faces are concealing, don't you? When a girl is being rejected she puts on an air that she doesn't care. She pretends that she is bored with the whole scene, while down deep inside she is experiencing awful, awesome pain. As those girls sat there, I stood to the side and watched them hurting for half the evening because no one asked them to dance.

When the dance was over, I was out on the street, joking and talking with some of my friends, when out of the gym came my science lab partner, Mary. Mary was a neat, neat girl; witty, humorous and, on top of that, she had mastered the art of ventriloquism. It is a very dangerous thing to sit next to a witty ventriloquist in a chemistry class.

For instance, one day the teacher said, 'We're going to have a test tomorrow.' I raised my hand and asked, 'What will it cover?' He said, 'Oh, whatever is on my mind.' Without moving her lips, Mary said in a husky voice, 'Then we don't have anything to worry about.' Everybody laughed and Mary looked at me as if to say, 'How could you say something like that, Tony?'

Mary was a terrific person, but she did not have the greatest figure in the world. She didn't have good-looking legs either. Our dating system is vicious to people who aren't shaped just right. That night Mary had been one of those girls who had spent the entire evening waiting, without luck, for someone to pay attention to her.

As she came out of the dance, Mary ran right by me. I tried to say, 'Hi!' but she didn't answer. She got into her father's waiting car and before he could pull away from the kerb, I watched her break down and start to cry.

I was furious. I was irate. I went into the principal's office the next day and said, 'No more for me. I'm finished with dances.' And he said, 'You can't allow your religion to come between you and your responsibilities.' I said, 'Hey, my minister really didn't understand what's wrong with dancing. He only saw the sexual thing. What I saw last night was cruelty. I saw some of my best friends and some of the neatest kids in our school getting hurt.'

Ask yourself this very simple question: 'How many young people do I know who are hurting because nobody ever asks them out?' You can find young people in any school every day who are hurting. And if you're going to act like a Christian, you will identify with those who hurt. You will feel their pain and their agony. I never went to another dance at the school. Not because I think dancing is wrong, but for another reason: I didn't want to be part of a system that hurts innocent people.

Whenever you create a system for teenagers that requires them to have partners of the opposite sex in order to participate, then you've created a social system or activity that automatically excludes a lot of kids. Furthermore, you end up excluding those who most need to be included. You close out those who are hurting the most. As Christians, we should be reaching out to the people whom society rejects. Instead, we sometimes unconsciously support a system which fosters their sense of rejection.

Jesus was committed to affirming those who were rejected by society. His life was an array of episodes in which he picked up people who were hurting and made them feel loved and significant. Jesus didn't exactly choose the most popular and attractive people to initiate His involvement. He said, 'From the stones the builder rejects will come the stones out of which I will build my new world.'

Here is the real issue: we have a dating system that glorifies the kids who are already glorified by our society and puts down the kids who are already put down. I feel bad for all of the Marys of the world. I think Christians should be agonizing over what our Western system of dating is doing to people.

I know some people are going to say that I'm overstating the case. They will argue that this system does not hurt kids. To such people I can only respond that you don't have to be a sociologist to see the hurts this system causes. Simple, honest observation will make this case.

A few years ago Janice Ian sold a million copies of a song. It was popular because it communicated the feelings of so many young people. Hurting teenagers listened intently whenever the song was played and thought to themselves, 'That's me. That song is about me.' The song goes like this:

I learned the truth at 17,
That love was meant for beauty queens
And high school girls with clear skin smiles.
While those of us with ravaged faces
Lacking in the social graces,
Desperately remained at home
Inventing lovers on the phone
Who called to say 'Come dance with me,'
And murmured vague obscenities,
It isn't all it seems, at 17,
For those of us who knew the pain
Of Valentines that never came
And those whose names were never called
When choosing sides for basketball,
It was long ago and far away
The world was younger than today,
And chains were all they gave for free
To ugly duckling girls like me, at 17.

The song tells it like it is and we Christians should be aware of that. The Western system of going out is hurting young people. If you go to a school with a thousand kids, the system usually works for only about two hundred of them. Only two hundred out of a thousand get the praise, the strokes and the recognition needed for a positive self-image. What about the other eight hundred who live their lives in 'quiet desperation'? Shouldn't Christians be heart-broken over them?

I know attractive, personable girls who leave secondary school never having been out with a boy, and those years without a boyfriend so devastate their sense of self-worth that they find themselves saying things like: 'I'm nothing. Nobody could love me.' The consequences of such self-contempt can destroy a girl's moral standards. Show me a girl with a lousy self-image and I'll show you a female who is very easy to sexually seduce. The female without a good self-concept is very easy to induce into having sex because she doesn't feel like she's worth anything. And when a girl begins to feel that she is junk, she begins to act like junk. A girl's self-concept has a powerful effect on her actions. If she thinks she's trash, she'll act like trash. On the contrary, if she thinks she's a precious child of God, she will act like one. We must do our utmost to ensure girls have the latter experience.

Going out as a group

The time has come for Christians to look for alternatives to our present dating system. Christians ought to invent and promote a new style of dating.

When I was teaching at the University of Pennsylvania, I became intrigued with a new style of dating that was emerging on the campus scene during the 1960s. They called it 'group dating.' Instead of boys and girls going off as pairs, a whole gang of kids would run around together. Instead of going to a movie or a sports event with just one person, about seven or eight boys and girls would go together. Nobody worried about who was linked with whom. All the kids simply had a good time together and enjoyed each other.

I think your youth group at church could do just that. Your youth group could be more than just a gathering on Sunday night after church. It could be more than a mini church service for young people. Your youth group could become a gang of kids who provide a social life for each other. Your youth group could turn into a fellowship of young kids who have fun with each other every Friday and Saturday night. It doesn't take much for something wonderful like that to happen to a youth group. All it takes is for somebody to speak for the group and say, 'Hey! Come along with us and have some fun. You don't have to go out with just one person. *Everybody* can come along with us. We want everybody to share. Let's have a good time together. It won't be as much fun without you.' You'll be surprised at the response to that kind of invitation.

I wish that you would make the following commitment: 'I no longer want just to go out with one person. I want to see a group of people going out together. It is all right for me to have a boyfriend or a girlfriend. But in social activities, I am going to make sure that everybody is invited, that everybody gets brought along, and that everybody participates. That's because it is a Christian obligation to reach out to the kids who feel left out and make them feel like they are included.'

Spirituality is caring about people who are left out, caring about people who are hurting. If you get so consumed in your own relationship with your boy-friend or girlfriend that you forget about all of the kids who are left out, you are not behaving like a Christian. We are supposed to be trying to tell people about the love of Jesus and there is no better way of doing that than by taking a kid who feels left out and giving him or her a sense of belonging to a group that cares. The love of God makes us brothers and sisters and an inclusive style for fun and recreation makes the feeling of 'family' very real.

Sex

We can't talk about dating without talking about sex. You knew I'd get to that eventually, didn't you? Here are some statistics: according to recent studies, 43 per cent of all girls leaving American secondary schools are sexually experienced. That means that they have had sexual intercourse. The percentage of American boys leaving secondary schools who have had sexual relations is even higher. Statistics like these are mind-boggling to those of us who grew up a generation ago.

As you might expect, the statistics for Christian young people who have had sexual relations are somewhat lower. But even those statistics are not as low as you might think. The figures for Americans show that 33 per cent of Christian females and approximately 40 per cent of Christian males engage in pre-marital sexual intercourse.

Some of you will ask with surprise, 'You aren't talking about born-again, Bible-believing Christians, are you?' As a sociologist who is also an evangelical

Christian, I've made a special study of our evangelical, Bible-believing kids and my studies show that that's just about where they fall – or fail. It seems that we are living in an age in which even people who consider themselves followers of Jesus Christ have become pretty loose, sexually speaking.

That is frightening for a variety of reasons. First of all, if you are a Christian, you have to be aware of the fact that Jesus Christ is *in* you. Jesus Christ is in you every minute of every day. You know what that means, don't you? It means that whenever you mess around, Jesus is involved in it with you. You can't leave Him outside the room when you mess around. You can't put Him out of your life temporarily because you want to do some things which you know will displease Him. When you are a Christian, He possesses you and involves Himself with all that you do. And so, when you do something degrading, or cheapen yourself in any way and then say, 'The only person affected by these actions of mine is me; I'm not hurting anybody else' – you are only kidding yourself. If Jesus is in you, then what you do not only affects you, it affects Jesus too. Makes sense, doesn't it? Try reading 1 Corinthians 6:15–17.

Secondly, Jesus is also in the other person. The person you might choose to use for your sexual games is also the temple of the Lord. There are a host of unexplored implications in the saying of Jesus in Matthew 25:40, which reminds us that whatever we do to another person we are doing to Jesus. Always realize that Jesus Christ is in you and that Jesus is in the other person at the same time. In any and all relations with others, Jesus is involved.

There is one last thing about sexual behaviour. The Bible says that we crucify Him anew each time we behave in a way that is contrary to His will. Sin is not simply breaking the law of God, it is re-crucifying Jesus. And that is meant to be taken literally.

One of my students once said to me, 'Look, I know I am sleeping around and I know it is wrong. But after all, I really believe that all of my sins were taken care of two thousand years ago on the cross. I live under the grace of God.' Believe it or not, that's really what he told me. He did what he did, knowing it was wrong but claiming that his sins were atoned for there and then on Calvary's cross. He did not grasp the fact that every time he bedded down with a pick-up, he crucified Jesus again. I wish that when that guy was doing his thing in bed he could hear the agonizing screams of Jesus. I wish he could hear Jesus crying and wailing. I wish he could experience what Jesus is going through at that very moment of what he is doing.

The Bible says, 'Do not sin that grace may abound.' Paul says, 'Recognize that you crucify Jesus daily.' Daily! So what am I saying? I'm saying this: if you are doing something that is obscene and if you are cheapening both yourself and your partner, you should also remember that at that very moment you are driving another nail into the hand of Jesus. You are once again lancing His side with a spear.

I am not saying that sex is obscene and dirty. Furthermore, I agree with the Freudian psychologists who claim that Victorian versions of Christianity have created unhealthy attitudes toward sexuality. Contrary to the Victorians, I am claiming that God has designed us for sexual enjoyment and that the gospel is good news for those who want to know how to maximize their sexual pleasures. The Bible outlines how this maximum gratification can be achieved: Allow sex to express love within the context of a binding relationship (i.e. marriage). The sexual act is not dirty, but it becomes dirty if it is carried out in a way that is contrary to what is prescribed by our Lord. When sex enhances a love relationship it is explosively wonderful.

Let me take a moment here to tell you about a way of messing around sexually that seems to be more common to Christians than to people who do not share Christian commandments. Christians, as I have said, are less likely to enter into sexual intercourse than non-Christians. However, while Christians may be less inclined to lose their virginity, they are the people who are most inclined to become what Alfred Kinsey, the great American sex researcher, called '*technical* virgins.' By 'technical virgin,' Kinsey meant a person who doesn't engage in sexual intercourse, but who does everything else. There are Christian young people who play with each other's sexual organs, neck in the nude, and mutually masturbate but do not 'go all the way.' In the midst of such circumstances, they try to kid themselves into believing that they are living within 'Christian limits' for sexual behaviour and are still 'saving themselves sexually' until marriage.

We don't often talk about petting in Christian circles. But there is an awful lot of 'very heavy sexual stuff' that goes on among Christian young people. It often gets so heavy that it diminishes their capability for spirituality and lessens their humanity. And even while such things are happening they demonstrate a 'technical self-righteousness' and applaud themselves because they haven't 'gone all the way.'

The reason I am going to such lengths in talking about sexual behaviour among young people is that I know all too well how sexual behaviour influences their thinking and belief systems. When I first came to teach at Eastern College, I was asked to be the chaplain for the college. Students often would come to my office, sit down and tell me that they had stopped believing in Jesus Christ. And I almost always knew why. They had stopped believing in Jesus because they had been compromising their sex lives. They would invariably say, 'Doctor, I no longer believe in Jesus because intellectually I find that the Christian faith is untenable.' I always used to say, 'And that is a lot of hogwash. Before we go any further in this discussion I want to ask you some questions about your sex life.'

I know enough about the Christian faith and enough about the arenas of the academic world to know that there is nothing intellectual which cannot ultimately be reconciled with the Christian faith. Christianity and valid intellectual insights can be put together and harmonized if one has the will to do so. I know that the reason most students become sceptical and give up their faith is usually unrelated to the academic process. As Blaise Pascal, the brilliant French intellectual of the sixteenth century once said, 'Doubt comes from disobedience.' If a Christian person is behaving sexually in a way that he or she knows is contrary to the will of God that behaviour creates cognitive dissonance. Good phrase, 'cognitive dissonance.' It means that there will be great inner tension when what a person does and tries to justify to the self is contrary to his or her established convictions.

There are two ways of resolving that guilt. Number one: a person can repent of the behaviour that he or she knows is contrary to his or her spiritual convictions and thus re-establish a sense of inner well-being. The other way to eliminate the cognitive dissonance and feel good again is for the person to reject the convictions that condemn his or her behaviour. To put it another way, a young person can get over guilt feelings if that person can put God out of his or her mind. If the person gets rid of God then he or she can do anything without feeling guilt – or cognitive dissonance. The person doesn't feel condemned once God has been put out of his or her life because there is no longer the awareness of one who will negatively judge sexual exploitation or any other kind of sin.

Most religious scepticism and loss of spirituality results, not through intellectual processes, but from disobeying what is known to be the will of God, particularly in sexual matters. I know more kids who have had their faiths destroyed through their sexual behaviour than by anything else. That is one reason why I plead with you so strongly to be faithful to Jesus in sexual matters and to recognize what is going on in your head when you mess around with your body.

Romance and love

Having said all this, I now want to talk about love. I know I've been talking a great deal about sex, but I want to turn our attention now to love.

I grew up on what this culture calls 'romantic love.' The pop songs back then created my perspective on love. The pop songs in my day were different from those of today. In my day, you understood the words (I'm sure you've heard that line from your parents). One of the most popular love songs when I was young went like this: 'Some enchanted evening, you will meet a stranger across a crowded room. And somehow you'll *know*.' So I grew up looking across crowded rooms. Romance was my thing. I believed what the songs said and was sure that one day I would meet somebody who would overwhelm me with a single glance.

Romance *does* happen. Instantaneous 'turn-ons' do occur. But love is deeper than romance. Romance is an on-off feeling. You know that. You probably have had several very intense romantic turn-ons by this stage of your life. While each of them was delicious at the time and while you swore to yourself it would last for ever, you must admit that it didn't last. It ended, and later on you had another turn-on with somebody else. Come on! Be honest! Isn't it true that two years ago you were head over heals in a romantic affair that you were sure would never end – and it did?

Whereas romance simply 'happens' and is an on-off affair, love must be created and it has a constancy about it. As the Bible says, 'Love never faileth.'

94

When I got married twenty-five years ago, I was very romantic, but I'm not sure I was a very loving husband. My wife will verify that I am much more loving today than I was on our wedding day, even though I may be somewhat less romantic.

One night we were coming home from New Jersey, zipping across Walt Whitman Bridge into Philadelphia, and my wife said, 'Look at us! *Look at us!'*

'What's the matter?' I asked.

She said, 'Look where you're sitting.'

I said, 'I am driving the car. When you are driving the car, it is best to sit behind the wheel.'

'Look at them?' she said, 'Look at them!'

So I looked into the car in front of us and there was this guy who looked like he had two heads. (You know what I mean, don't you?)

We crossed the bridge into Philadelphia and all the while I was aware that my wife was all upset because we weren't as romantic as we once had been. As we drove through the city we travelled through Fairmount Park. I noticed a parking place for lovers. It was located right on the river-bank. It was perfect. I stopped the car, switched off the ignition, turned on the parking lights (fortunately the kids were still asleep in the back seat), reached out and grabbed my wife, pulled her over (and smashed her head on the steering wheel). And she said, 'What are you doing?'

I said, 'I'm being romantic.'

She said, 'Take me home!'

So much for being romantic. Romance is nice stuff, and it does happen. It happens often but it should not be trusted. I must admit that I often have romantic turn-ons – but I try not to take them seriously.

You're thinking, 'Campolo, you're an old man of 48. You're bald. You ought to be beyond all that sort of thing.' Not at all. The old motor's still running. I often have romantic fantasies. I'm not proud of that fact. But such things do happen to me. Yes! Even at my age.

You are naive if you think that once you accept Jesus you are not going to experience these kinds of emotional reactions any more. If you believe that, you are going to be very vulnerable to Satan, because nobody is in a more precarious position than the individual who thinks he or she is spiritually safe and secure. The person who believes that he or she can't be seduced is the one who is most likely to get blown away.

What Christians should recognize is that there is a deeper kind of love than romance. The ancient Greeks called it *philos*. It's the kind of love that grows up between two people who have the same goals and commitments in life. It's a love that grows up between two people who are working towards something they both hold dear. This is the kind of love which Christians should create in their relationships. This kind of love goes much deeper than romance.

Imagine a triangle. Along the base of the triangle are all the things that you say are important to you. As you move toward the apex of the triangle, the base will get smaller and smaller, leaving room for fewer and fewer things. Eventually, there is room for only one thing. Then you have to answer this question: 'What is that one thing that you will hold on to after you have sacrificed everything else?' What is your ultimate concern? What is that for which you would die? Once you have defined what is so important to you that you are willing to sacrifice everything else to hold on to it, you ought to look for somebody else who has the same commitment.

If you are a Christian, by definition you are somebody who is committed to Jesus; you are someone who says from the depths of your being, 'For me to live is Christ, to die is gain.' You are ready to live for Jesus 100 per cent. Consequently, if you are a Christian, and you want to experience this deeper kind of love called *philos*, you must marry someone who shares your commitment to Jesus. As each of you grows closer to Jesus you will simultaneously grow closer and closer to each other. That is why the Bible tells us, 'Be not unequally yoked with unbelievers.' In the Old Testament, the Bible asks, 'Can two walk together unless they be agreed?' For a love relationship to work over the long haul it is essential for you and your partner to agree on a purpose for life. It is essential that you both believe the same things about Christ.

All too seldom when kids are dating do they carry on philosophical discussions. You're thinking, 'Philosophical discussions – you've got to be kidding! Where are you at, Tony baby?!' Hey, the most important thing you can do with your partner is to find out where that other person is coming from and where he or she is going. Be sure to discuss your commitments together. If the two of you are not committed to the same things, you will not be able to develop a commitment to each other.

I remember so well a certain young woman at Eastern College who had committed herself to be a missionary with Wycliffe Bible Translators. She had been going out with a guy named John and one day she came into my office with tears running down her cheeks. She sat down and buried her head in her hands. With concern and perplexity, I asked, 'What's the matter?'

She said, 'John wants to marry me.'

'You like him, don't you?' I asked.

She said, 'I'm crazy about John.'

'Well, then, what's the problem? You love John. John wants to marry you. Sounds perfect.'

'John is not committed to Jesus,' she answered. 'He doesn't share my commitment to go as a missionary to Brazil.'

'What are you going to do?' I asked.

Her eyes narrowed as she looked at me and said, 'You know what I'm going to do. I'm going to Brazil as a missionary. I just came in here for you to pray with me – and cry with me.'

And I did both.

One Friday afternoon John and I got into a car, drove that young woman to Kennedy Airport in New York and put her on a plane to fly to Brazil. When she boarded that plane she was crying, John was crying, and I was crying. And as she flew away, I thought to myself, 'Is this what it means to be a follower of Christ? Is this what it means to be a disciple of our Lord?' And the answer is, 'You bet your life.'

Jesus says, 'Unless you love me more than you love your mother, your father, your sister or your brother, you are not worthy of me.' You can't be a follower of Jesus unless you are into that.

I can give you another case in which the result of a love relationship was a rejection of the Lord's will. A couple came to me to be married. I knew the young woman well. She had made a commitment to Christ in a Bible study group I had led. Her fiancé was a complete stranger to me. When I asked him if he was a Christian, he coolly announced that he had once believed in God but had 'grown out of that sort of thing.'

I asked the young woman if she was going to marry him in spite of the fact that he wasn't a Christian. She angrily replied, 'Don't go quoting the Bible to me, Campolo. You're always quoting the Bible.' I don't know what she thought I was going to quote. Shakespeare? She went on, 'You're probably going to quote that verse, "Be not unequally yoked to unbelievers," aren't you? Don't you understand? I love him, and nothing is going to stand in the way of our being together.'

I told her that she could not be a true Christian unless she loved Jesus more than she loved her fiancé, but she would not listen. However, something did get in the way of the two of them being together for the rest of their lives. They got divorced. I don't think a marriage can work if its's built upon the necessity of going against the known will of God.

Christian lovers are people who know there is a kind of love different from the romance that this society calls love. Christian lovers know there is a kind of love that comes into their lives, possesses them, and allows Jesus to flow through them into the lives of the other person. In such a relationship, each Christian lover knows that Jesus wants to love the

YOU CAN MAKE A DIFFERENCE

other person through him or her. I call upon you to be Christian lovers.

There is a children's story that I have loved for a long time, and it still moves me every time I read it. It is called *The Velveteen Rabbit* and was written by Marjorie Williams. In one passage, a toy rabbit and a toy horse are talking to each other. Their conversation, which I believe communicates a great deal of truth, goes like this:

'What is REAL?' asked the Rabbit one day, as they were lying side by side near the nursery fender, just before Nana came in to tidy up the room. 'Does it mean having things that buzz inside you and a stick-out handle?'

'Real isn't how you are made,' said the Skin Horse. 'It's a thing that happens to you. When a child loves you for a long, long time, not just to play with, but REALLY loves you, then you become Real.'

'Does it hurt?' asked the Rabbit.

'Sometimes,' said the Skin Horse, for he was always truthful. 'When you are Real, you don't mind being hurt.'

'Does it happen all at once, like being wound up,' he asked, 'or bit by bit?'

'It doesn't happen all at once,' said the Skin Horse. 'You become. It takes a long time. That's why it doesn't often happen to people who break easily, or have sharp edges, or who have to be carefully kept. Generally, by the time you are Real, most of your hair has been loved off, and your eyes drop out and you get loose in the joints and very shabby. But these things don't matter at all, because once you are Real, you can't be ugly except to people who don't understand.'

What I have described to you is so much deeper than romance, and this is what Jesus wants for you. He wants you to have a relationship in which you and your partner become more alive, more real, more vital. When you have that kind of relationship, it creates a sense of excitement, a sense of euphoria, an unspeakable joy. When you are turned on to somebody who shares the same commitment that you do, then you are in love with somebody who is in love with the same Jesus that you love. When both you and your partner can say, 'We are going to serve Jesus Christ together,' you will have an explosive excitement that will make your life together all that you hoped it would be.

When relationships break up

In most dating relationships, there are times when you feel like breaking up and there may come a time when you do have to break up. If that time comes in your relationship, please, please handle it with honesty. I find that a lot of Christian kids refuse to be honest in such situations.

Too often when a girl wants to break off with a guy, she just doesn't tell him. Instead she thinks that it is better to make life miserable for him. She thinks that if she hurts him enough, he will break off with her and then she won't have to do the dirty work. Of course it happens the other way round, as well. There are guys who utilize the same strategy when they break off relationships with girls.

I have seen kids hurt each other so much in the process of breaking off that after their romantic relationship is over, they can't even be friends any more. You see that all around you every day in school, don't you? You know kids who used to be 'in love' but who don't even speak to each other any more. The Bible teaches, 'Be ye kind one to another; tenderhearted, forgiving one another, even as God for Christ's sake has forgiven you.' Are you kind to the people you go out with?

I'm old enough to remember Elvis Presley singing, 'Don't Be Cruel.' There is so much cruelty among young people in today's world. And I have seen too many Christian young people who are cruel in the ways that they end romantic relationships. I call you to be kind and honest in the process of breaking up.

Staying single

Some of you reading this book will have to face the possibility of remaining single. There will be a signficant number of you who will not get married. Perhaps you may find yourself in a place where you either have to choose between marrying somebody who doesn't believe what you believe and doesn't share your committments, or not getting married at all. That is a hard choice to face, but I must tell you that there are a lot of things worse than being single the rest of your life. One of those is being married to someone with whom you do not have a camaraderie in the things of God.

I ask you to recognize that you may be asked to accept singleness if you follow Jesus. But nobody ever said that following Jesus would be easy. On the other hand, singleness can be a blessing. It can allow a person to serve Jesus in a way that is impossible for married people. The apostle Paul writes in 1 Corinthians 7:32–34:

> I would like you to be free from concern. An unmarried man is concerned about the Lord's affairs – how he can please the Lord. But a married man is concerned about the affairs of this world – how he can please his wife – and his interests are divided. An unmarried woman or virgin is concerned about the Lord's affairs: Her aim is to be devoted to the Lord in both body and spirit. But a married woman is concerned about the affairs of this world – how she can please her husband (NIV).

Paul makes clear what anybody who has been to the mission field knows: The unencumbered state of single Christian workers makes them capable of doing things for Jesus that married people can never do. Single people can live in places where married people with children do not feel they should raise those children. They are able to move from place to place as needs arise, with a minimum of difficulty. They require very little money for support. And they have more time to devote to those whom God has called them to serve. Singleness should not be viewed as a punishment to be endured, but as an opportunity for vast possibilities of service.

Surrendering your life to Jesus

I am calling upon you to surrender your life to Jesus. This requires that you order your boyfriends or girlfriends, your sex life, marriage or state of singleness in accordance with His will. If I were to ask you to give your money to Jesus, I have a feeling that you might do that. If I asked you to give some time to Jesus, most of you would do that, too. But I am asking for something deeper than that. I'm asking you to say from the depths of your heart, 'Jesus, I am going to let you govern my life with members of the opposite sex. I am going to behave when I go out with people in a way that will meet your approval. I am going to be sensitive to the kids who are hurting and left out. I am going to commit myself only to people who share my commitments to you, because I know that you want me to have a love relationship that will make me real. I will accept singleness as an opportunity for greater service if you give me the special grace to overcome my sexual longings.'

Will you do it? Will you give your love life over to Jesus and trust Him that His way of doing things is the best way? I sure hope so. More than that, I pray so.

DISCIPLESHIP
Living Life to the nth Degree

4

Priorities in discipleship

In this chapter I'm going to talk to you about how to stay a Christian. The problem I'm dealing with is maintenance. Studies indicate that not all of the people who come down the aisle at evangelistic meetings remain Christians. You know that many of the people who say that they have made a commitment to Jesus fall by the wayside. I don't know what the theological implications of these realities might be and I leave it to the theologians to fight over the possibilities of whether or not one can stop being a Christian. But I do know that Jesus made clear that not all those who receive His word become fruitful servants of God. Read Matthew 13 if you want proof of what I say. In my experience, a survey of people who have made public commitments to Jesus would reveal that many of them, ten years later, have little to do with the church or the Christian lifestyle. There is a tremendous loss of people who make a decision for Jesus Christ, but who do not follow it through.

Whenever I address young people and have them respond to my invitation to follow Jesus, I usually experience a strange kind of depression. The depression results from the fact that I know that a significant proportion of them will not be walking with Jesus ten years later. And the reason they will not be walking with Jesus is that they will not have done the things I am going to suggest that you do in the next few pages. If new converts would follow these suggestions, I could almost guarantee that they would be in step with Christ for the rest of their lives. I hope that you will give careful attention to these biblically pre-scribed instructions which I believe to be essential for the maintenance of the Christian life.

Bible study is essential

The first thing in maintaining yourself as a Christian is to recognize that you've got to get into Bible study. You knew I was going to say that, didn't you? I know that when you read the Bible it sometimes gets pretty boring. You and I may as well admit that right now. However one reason Bible reading might seem boring could be that you don't read it properly.

My mistake when I began to read the Bible was that I started at Genesis and tried to read the whole Bible through from the beginning to the end. Genesis was OK, but when I got to Leviticus and everybody was 'begatting' somebody else in those incredible geneaologies, that's when it really got me. And that's when I tended to give up on the whole project. I would make promises, usually at summer camp, to read the Bible. I'd say, 'God, I promise to read a chapter a day to keep the devil away,' or something like that. But reading the Bible just never seemed to be an ongoing proposition with me. If I had got some decent instructions about *how* to go about daily Bible reading, it might have been different. That's why I am so eager to give some direction to you. Perhaps your Bible reading time will go better than mine did when I was your age.

The first thing about reading the Bible is that you've got to know Jesus. You have to have a personal relationship with Him. Only then will the Bible have the kind of excitement about it that will leave you wanting read more of it.

When I went off to college, my mother gave me a book called *The Silver Trumpet*. It was written by a man named J. Wesley Ingles. I read it and I thought it was a pretty good book, but it didn't blow me away or do anything special to me. Then at the end of my first term at college, I re-read the book. The second time I read it, that book had an aliveness and a power to it that it lacked in the first reading. Why? What caused the change? The answer can be found in the fact that during my first year my English teacher had been J. Wesley Ingles, the author of that book. The man who had written it was my teacher and the fact that I knew the author made all the difference in the world when I read the book.

The reason the Bible doesn't come alive to many people is that they don't know the Author personally. If that's your problem, why not get to know the Author of the Bible right now? Jesus is there with you. He wants to become your personal friend. All you have to do is say within yourself as deeply as you know how, 'Jesus, I want you to be my personal friend. I want you to come into my life. I want you to possess me.'

Ask Him to come into your life and He will. The Bible says that He stands at the door of your heart and knocks. The Scriptures teach that if you'll just say, 'OK, come in and take possession of me,' He will do it. He will come in and take possession of you. When that happens He will equip you to understand the Scriptures in a way that otherwise would have been impossible. The Holy Spirit, who is Jesus spiritually present with you, interprets the Scripture for you as you read it. When you are under the Spirit's direction the Bible's meaning for you will become clear and powerful. You can buy a thousand commentaries, you can go to a hundred Bible Studies, but nothing will help you to understand what the Bible is saying more than the presence of the Holy Spirit in your life. This is the first thing you've go to know.

Secondly, you've got to have an orderly progression in your study of the Bible. Let me suggest that you begin by reading the Gospel of Mark. It would be great if you would say, 'This year I am going to read the Gospel of Mark through twenty times.' Why twenty times? Because I think that it is more important to know the Gospel of Mark through and through, inside out, than just to read the Bible through superficially.

Every once in a while someone tells me proudly, 'I've just finished reading the Bible through from cover to cover.' I feel like asking that person, 'how much of it do you remember? Did it affect you while you were reading it? Did you savour and ponder its words or did your just read for the sake of reading it?'

I want you to know the Gospel of Mark so well that if somebody asks, 'Hey! What does the Bible say about material wealth?' You can say, 'Let me quote to you from the tenth chapter of Mark.' And right away you'll be able to quote the relevant passage about the rich young ruler. I believe you ought to read Mark and read it again and read it again, and that you ought to memorize whole sections of it if you can.

Scholars tell us that Mark served as a kind of director of religious education among Christians in the early church. Paul would win people to Jesus and Barnabas would pastor them, but it was Mark's job to teach new converts that they needed to know about the life of Jesus. Some biblical scholars suggest that first century Christians were required – are you ready for this? – to memorize what is now the entire book of Mark. That was one of the ways in which they were discipled into the church.

The Gospel of Mark was written to provide a basis to help new Christians become acquainted with the most important elements of the life and teachings of Jesus. That is why I am suggesting it to you. The Gospel of Mark was good for young Christians in the first century, so it ought to be good for you if you are just staring out in your Christian walk. Read it through and learn it in depth.

After the book of Mark, I would suggest that you study the epistle of James. Read James through ten, fifteen or twenty times until you know *it* backwards, forwards and inside out too. The book of James talks about very practical things that you really need to know. It covers topics like gossiping, how to use your money, how to treat people and how to act towards your parents. All kinds of important things are outlined in James.

I hope that I've made it clear that the way to study the Bible is to go at it one book at a time. That has been my style and it has served me well. Right now I am really pushing through the epistle to the Ephesians. That's my book for this year and I guarantee you that by the end of this year, I'm going to *know* the epistle to the Ephesians. I hope you will adopt an 'in depth' style of Bible reading and abandon the kind of superficial reading that characterizes the Bible study of too many Christians.

Prayer is essential

The second thing you've got to get into is prayer. Here is something that too few of us do very well. It isn't enough to get into praying when we want something – like just before an exam at school. Many people get very spiritual when a test paper stares them in the face. Then they pray, 'God, give me the answers. I know I've never looked at a book; but Lord, you are able to transform things. You are able to transfer the knowledge from the book into my head and onto the paper. Please, Jesus, do it – that I might be faithful to you.' But most of the time it doesn't work to pray when you haven't studied – at least it never worked for me.

Then some of you are like my own boy. When he was still very little, he came into the living room one night and said, 'I'm going to bed, and I'm going to be praying. Anybody want anything?' (I love it!) You act as if prayer is a way of getting whatever you want, regardless of how self-centred your request might be. Too often we treat prayer as though it is a time when we can read off a list of non-negotiable demands to the Almighty.

It is intriguing to note that the Bible says that the Lord knows what we have need of before we even ask. For instance, when we say, 'Dear Lord Sister Mary is ill in hospital,' the Lord is not saying, 'Oh, I didn't know that! Thanks for filling me in, Tony.'

God is God and He knows what you need before you ask. Now that statement may leave you wondering, 'So why even ask?' I've often wondered about that myself. If God knows what we need before we ask, why do we even have to bother to ask? The answer is simple. We need to make our requests known to God, not because it is neccessary to inform Him of our needs, but because we need to establish what theologians call 'a relationship of dependency' with God. We need to tell God what we need, not because God is ignorant of our needs, but because we need to know that we are dependent upon Jesus for everything.

One of my non-Christian friends claims that he rejects Christianity because it makes people depend upon God when they should depend upon themselves. He claims that Christianity is a crutch for weak people and makes them less than self-sufficient. What my friend does not realize is how weak we humans really are. He is deceived if he thinks that we can solve the ultimate problems of our lives without being dependent upon God. We all need to lean on something. Frankly, I'm relieved, more than words can express, that Jesus says, 'Come, lean on me.' Lean on the everlasting arms. That's what prayer is all about. It's taking time to lean on Jesus. It's acknowledging that without God we can do nothing.

When we come to God in prayer, He invites us to talk to Him in an intimate manner. There is a time and a place for the formal types of prayer that they teach ministers at theological colleges and which characterize church liturgies. And if a formal prayer is required, I know how to deliver one. Try this one for example:

> Oh, Thou great Creator of the universe. Oh, Thou who doth provide us with every good and perfect gift. Oh, Thou who doth give us the sun in the morning and the stars at night. We beseech Thee to be present and bless us on this occasion.

I hope you're impressed.

On the other hand, consider this: I have a twenty-year-old son, and I cannot imagine him walking into our house and saying to me, 'Oh, thou chairman of the sociology department at Eastern College, Oh thou who doth clothe me, feed me and provide me with every good and perfect gift; I beseech thee this day, lend me the car.' That's not the way he talks to me. I'm his daddy. So, like a good Italian boy, he walks into the house, throws his arms around me, kisses me and says, 'Hi Dad, can I borrow the car?' You see, we love each other.

Jesus wants each of us to be intimate with Him. That is why the apostle Paul tells us in the eighth chapter of Romans that we should not pray as people filled with fear, but we should talk to God as one who is closer than any father could ever be. Actually, the apostle Paul instructs us to address God as 'Abba,' which is the ancient Hebrew word for 'daddy.' There is no one who wants to be closer to you than Jesus does. He doesn't want to be regarded as some transcendental Shylock, demanding his pound of flesh. He wants to be intimate with you. Be sure to talk to Jesus with the intense love and intimacy which He desires from you.

There's one more thing I want to tell you about praying. And that is that when we pray we should allow God time to answer. Too often we pray and pray and pray, and we do all the talking. Then when we are finished talking, we end the prayer. We leave no time for God to speak to us.

Suppose I called you on the telephone and I said, 'Glenn (or whatever your name is), how are you doing? I'm really looking forward to being in town and seeing you. It's going to be nice being your guest. We are going to have a great time together, aren't we? See you then.' Then, without giving you a chance to reply, I hung up, turned to my wife and said, 'Funny thing about Glenn. He's a nice guy, but he never speaks to me!' My wife would say, 'Speak to you? You never gave him a chance to talk!'

Isn't that the way we treat God? We never give Him a chance to speak to us either. We talk, talk, talk and after we finish telling God what He already knows, we hang up. Right? We say, 'I ask these things in Jesus' name, Amen.' Full stop. Dialling tone. It must be frustrating to be God. Just when He hopes that we will listen to Him – we hang up on Him.

Let God speak to you

The Bible says, 'Be still and know that I am God.' Another way of translating that – the 'Authorized Tony Campolo Translation' – is, 'Shut up! Knock it off and let me speak to you!' Each of us must learn the art of being silent and letting God speak. It took me a long time before I was able to be inwardly still so that God could speak to me. But contrary to some opinions, God does speak to people. The problem is that most of us don't give Him a chance to speak. We think that God does not personally address us, when, in reality, we fail to take the steps to create the situation in which we can become sensitive to Him.

It takes me about fifteen to twenty minutes to get ready before God can speak to me, because it takes me that long to become still. Inwardly still. It takes me between fifteen and twenty minutes before all the noise that is running round in my mind dies down and I become inwardly quiet. Only then do I begin to experience inner stillness. Only when I am inwardly quiet do I begin to sense God speaking to me.

The Scriptures say that God doesn't have a voice that is loud like thunder. His voice is not like a roaring fire. The Bible says that when God speaks, it is in a still soft voice. That implies that only those who are inwardly quiet can receive His messages. When I wait in silence, God does speak to me. His messages do not come in words, but in feelings. Like 'the rumblings of deep waters,' I sense Him moving in the depths of my being. I can't tell you how many times I have gone to prayer confused and upset, and have found in the stillness a God who gives me a peace that passes all understanding. I can't begin to tell you how many times I have gone to prayer confused and frustrated and found in God a sense of direction, a sense of purpose, a sense of calm.

Prayer is incredibly essential. It is through prayer that one gets a sense of being led by God, a sense of being guided by God, and a sense of God's direction for life. The Bible says, 'As many as are led by the Spirit of God, they are the children of God.' Through prayer one gets that leading.

There are two ways that I can tell you how to get to my house near Philadelphia. I can draw you a map, give it to you and say, 'Go ahead, follow this map.' You may or may not get there.

The other thing I can do is to say, 'Get in the car and I will come along with you. I will show you how to get from here to there. I will guide you every inch of the way. I will tell you where to turn and I will tell you what route to take. Instead of a map, I will give you my presence.'

God does something like the latter. He doesn't provide a road-map that lays out the path of your life from beginning to end. Instead, He says, 'I'll go with you all the way. I'll direct you as we go along. I'll keep you on the way you should go. Through prayer I will help you to sense the path I want you to follow.'

Every once in a while some student comes to me and says, 'I want to discover the will of God for my life.' Now I haven't the slightest idea how to do that. Nowhere in the Bible does it say that God is going to give you a plan for your entire life. He never said that He would lay out His plan for your life in cinemascope so you can view it in its entirety. What He does promise is to lead you *as you go;* to direct you day by day; to show you His will hour by hour. If you are sensitive to Him, sensitive to His leading – and that is what prayer is all about – He promises to guide you personally every step of the way.

I assure you that I had no idea ten years ago that I would be doing what I am doing today. And I have no idea where God wants me to be ten years from now. But that doesn't upset me. I trust God and believe that He will take care of me. I feel like He's saying to me, 'You will sense through prayer where I want to take you and you can rest assured that everything will turn out to be good for you.' I can take him at His word when He says, 'If you are willing to listen to me and to be led by my Spirit, you will be my child and and I will abide with you for ever.

A support group is essential

At this point in our discussion, I want to talk to you about how to stay faithful in your commitment to grow spiritually. I want to share with you a very important lesson that I have learned about how to keep up my personal Bible study and maintain a personal prayer life. Until I learned this lesson, my Christian growth pattern was very much an on-off thing. After hearing some inspirational speaker or attending a Christian conference, I would be very devoted to Bible reading and prayer. But after a few weeks, I would slip away from a pattern of daily devotions and quiet time. As many times as I promised God that this would not happen, it would happen. I couldn't be trusted to maintain a faithful lifestyle. Then I learned this lesson: Nobody can be trusted to maintain a life of dedication to a Christian lifestyle without the support of others. No one can remain committed without a support group. It took me a long time to realize that I needed some brothers in Christ to assume responsibility for my spiritual development.

A few years ago I got together with three other guys and we formed a *support group*. These three friends meet with me on Thursday mornings and for a couple of hours we talk together, pray together and joke with each other. We tell each other what is going on in our respective lives. We talk about our problems. We provide encouragement for each other and correct each other. It is this small group that excites me and keeps me alive spiritually. Unless each of you gets into some kind of support group, I don't think you're going to make it as a Christian. I don't think you're going to be consistently faithful. I don't think you're going to stay alive spiritually.

The problem for most young people is that they all have had their experiences in their lives when they have had intense spiritual experiences. You remember them. Perhaps it was at some Christian camp and the scene was like this: Everybody was sitting round the camp-fire having just sung a thousand verses of 'Kum-Ba-Yah.' The speaker, who had given the devotional messages all week long, was starting his last talk with the hope of getting the campers to make commitments to Christ. He probably said, 'Kids we've had a really good time this week, haven't we?' With that, everyone looks sweetly at each other.

'We've come to really care about each other, too.'

People start holding hands.

Then he pulls this one: 'You know, gang, this is probably the last time we'll ever be together like this.' That does it. A hundred kids start crying simultaneously.

His next line is predictable. 'OK, gang, you're alive in Jesus now, but are you going to be alive a week from now? Two weeks from now? It is easy to be a Christian when you are up here on the mountain-top, but what about when you are back at school? What will you be like when you're down in the valley after this summer camp is over?'

In such a setting, you and most of the other kids round the camp-fire made decisions to follow Jesus. You made decisions to read the Bible daily and to pray. You were sure you would never lose the spiritual aliveness of that moment – but you did.

Or perhaps your commitment was made at a special evangelistic meeting at church. You went down the aisle when the preacher gave the invitation. You were taken from the sanctuary into a prayer room where a counsellor prayed with you and you promised God that you would do those things essential for spiritual growth and development – but you failed to keep your promise.

Knowing God's power

There was once a man who could be counted on to go down the aisle at evangelistic meetings in order to recommit his life to Christ. Each time he would get down on his knees at the altar and yell, 'Fill me, Jesus! Fill me, Jesus!' He'd get all psyched up with religion, but three weeks later he would lose his excitement and be right back in the same old worldy ways. Every time a new evangelist hit town and held meetings, the man would go through the same routine. He'd go down the aisle, get down on his knees at the altar and shout over and over again, 'Fill me, Jesus!' People became cynical about his commitments at the altar, and one time when he was doing his thing and yelling, 'Fill me, Jesus!' some lady at the back of the church shouted, 'Don't do it, Lord! He leaks!'

That is one of the great problems of Christian life, isn't it? We leak. All of us have had some super-duper spiritual experience in which we felt close to God, but soon found out that it didn't last. All of us feel like we leak. We seem to lose our zeal and excitement. All of us fail to carry out faithfully the commitments we have made to do the will of God.

To make the situation more problematic, there's always some joker who stupidly says, 'Yeah, but if it had been a real experience with God in the first place it would have lasted.' Which naturally leads you to believe your experience wasn't real. Don't be deceived. Even a *real* spiritual experience will not last. We all lose it. We *all* leak.

Well, then, what's the answer? How does a person keep from leaking? The bad news is that we can't stop the leaking. The good news is that each of us can be refilled regularly. Being regularly refilled is what Jesus wants for us. He doesn't expect you and me to have some kind of super-spiritual one-time filling with His Spirit to last us for the rest of our lives. Instead, he wants us to be *constantly refilled* with the

Holy Spirit. And that is why each of us must be part of a small support group.

The primary function of a support group is to regularly provide spiritual renewal for its members. That's what my group does for me. They fill me, they enliven me. What they do for me each Thursday morning is to bring me back to life. The world literally kills me. My spirit becomes deadened through my interactions with so many people I meet in my daily round of activities, but that group brings me back to life.

I know you've heard of the Holy Spirit. That same God who came down and lived in Jesus Christ two thousand years ago, is present with us today as one called the Holy Spirit. And as the Holy Spirit, God can become a powerful Presence in our lives. However, many of us fail to realize that one of the best ways to become receptive to the infilling of the Holy Spirit is through the conditions created by the fellowship of a support group. The Scripture says, 'Where two or three are gathered together in my name, there am I in the midst of them.' The Bible is telling us that the Spirit of God becomes a dynamic Presence when a support group gets together in the name of Jesus and seeks the spiritual renewal He promises to all who gather together in His name.

Knowing God's presence

One morning I got together with the members of my group just before taking a trip to Chicago. It was one of those times when we were sharing and talking on a very deep level, and I felt the Spirit of God flow into me and enrich me. I felt alive and powerful as my friends renewed me spiritually. I knew I had been refilled with the Spirit when I left that meeting. I went to the Philadelphia airport to catch the plane to Chicago, still feeling a glowing sensation derived from my support group. When I got on the plane, I found myself next to a businessman who obviously was very upset. There are few things as scary as being on an aeroplane seated next to a nervous man. You always wonder whether he knows something you don't know.

I wanted to share Jesus with that poor guy, but I didn't know how to start the conversation. I wanted to tell him that Jesus could help him, but I didn't know how to go about it. Suddenly, I felt that the Lord was leading me to do something that you might think is peculiar. I focused my mind on that man. You can call it telepathy, you can it ESP, you can call it anything you like, but I just mentally zapped him. I focused all of my spiritual power on him. I closed my eyes and mentally concentrated on him. Over and over I kept focusing the name of 'Jesus' on him. Without saying a word, I tried to communicate the love of Jesus to that man. My support group had empowered me and I was giving the power derived from my group to this stranger. I sat there and bombarded his mind with Jesus all the way to Chicago. I focused 'Jesus' on him the whole trip.

When the plane touched down in Chicago, I prayed, 'Lord, I have been sharing you with this guy for the last two hours. If you want me to talk to him, give me a sign.' With that, he nudged me and said, 'Mister, I've got problems and I want to talk to you. I think you can tell me about God.' What is amazing is that I wasn't surprised. I *expected* him to make that move. After all, I had been focusing the Holy Spirit on him for two whole hours.

The two of us went into the airport terminal and over cups of hot chocolate, talked about spiritual things for a long time. When we were through, he accepted the Lord. He responded to the invitation to allow Jesus to become Lord of his life. I believe that he became a Christian because my support group had equipped me to minister to him in the power of the Holy Spirit even when the words were not being uttered. I believe that the power of the Holy Spirit derived from fellowship with my three friends empowered me to enable that man to experience the presence of Jesus in a very special way. I believe that my non-verbal communication with him made him ready for what I would say to him.

Knowing God's wisdom

Too many times when we want to share Jesus with somebody, we try to do it with clever words. We think that if we've got the right words or the right technique, we can win people to the Lord. Some of us think that all we have to do is take some course and learn the correct approach to witnessing and people will respond to us. But if all we come with is a Bible verse or a memorized technique, we're going to fail. The Four Spiritual Laws are one of the best tools for evangelism – but they're simply not enough. The apostle Paul once said, 'I come to you not simply with excellency of words, but I come to you in the power of the Holy Spirit.' We too must learn that the good words are effective in evangelistic outreach only if they are undergirded with the Spirit of God.

The Bible says, 'I am not ashamed of the gospel of Christ, for it is the *power* of God unto salvation.' God wants to empower you, but there is a great likelihood that you are not going to have His power unless you belong to a little support group. This is the point that I am trying very hard to make: *Jesus empowers you through fellowship.* If you were reading this as part of a class assignment, I would make you write that down and underline it: *Jesus empowers you through fellowship.*

I want you to form a support group with two or three of your friends. Choose people whose company you enjoy and with whom you have a lot in common. Ask these people if they would be willing to enter into a covenant with you. The members of this group must be willing to care for one another and assume responsibility for one another in spiritual matters.

Jesus had such a group, didn't He? You can name them. His little support group was composed of Peter, James and John. Whenever Jesus needed to be empowered, He got together with them. They were with Him on the Mount of Transfiguration. They were with Him when He needed friendship. He called them to be with Him in His hour of deepest prayer in Gethsemane. And when they fell asleep instead of lending Him their support, He was sorely disappointed.

Some of you are thinking, 'Wait a minute! He was God!' Yes, but He was God incarnated with the limitations of human flesh. All that Jesus did, He did within the same limitations that each of us experience as human beings. He did His mighty works through prayer, and He modelled for us in His fellowship with His disciples the kind of relationship out of which spiritual power grows. Jesus never performed any miracles in His own strength. Every miracle He performed, He performed in the power of the Father who sent Him. And He demonstrated how that power can be available to each of us. He showed us that getting together in His name can provide the kind of fellowship in which His power can be experienced.

It used to be that when I strayed away from Jesus, I didn't know how to get back. I'd go to my pastor and say, 'I can't pray.'

My pastor would respond, 'When you can't pray, pray.'

That didn't make any sense to me. So I'd think maybe he wasn't hearing me right.

'I can't pray,' I would say again.

And he would answer, 'Pray. The more you can't pray, the more you need to pray.'

Today I have a good answer to the question of what to do at those times in life when I feel so devoid of the presence of God that praying seems impossible. When those times come, I depend on the three friends in my support group to get me back into a right relationship with Jesus. I don't have to depend on my own prayers to restore my empty soul. I can depend on my three friends to do that. They are responsible for me. If I am not close to Jesus, it is their fault. I have said to them, 'You are responsible for where I am spiritually, even as I am responsible for each of you spiritually.' We are mutually supportive. We believe that we are responsible to 'bear each other's burdens' (Galatians 6:2).

Every Christian also needs a group to hold him or her accountable for his or her behaviour. Whenever my life gets messed up, my friends immediately call an emergency meeting to straighten me out. They say, 'Campolo, there are certain things in your life that are screwed up, things that are contrary to the will of God, and we are here to correct you.' If they didn't do that for me, I could stray away from God without even realizing I was doing so. Without their correcting ministry I could mess up my life with ease. Each member of our group is responsible for the way the other members of the group live out their discipleship.

Do you have a support group to which you are accountable? If not, let me say this as directly as I know how: *Without such a small support group, you are not likely to survive spiritually.*

Belonging to a church is essential

The last thing that I want you to recognize as being essential to spiritual growth and maturity is membership in a local church. You need to belong to a church. I have to say that because so many people have become negative towards the church. Indeed, there is much to criticize about the institutional church. Pointing out the shortcomings of some local congregations is easy to do. You and I know what is wrong with the church.

I know this sounds harsh and I'm not writing it to knock anybody in particular, but these religious institutions have no right to spend millions of pounds on buildings when half the world is starving to death. There is something wrong when we spend more money on stained glass windows than we spend on feeding the hungry kids in Bangladesh. I admit that the institutional church really has its priorities messed up in a lot of other ways, too. However, I still love the institutional church and I am committed to its ministry in the world. Furthermore, I believe that Jesus loves the institutional church and weeps when she fails to realize her potential.

Actually, I tried to be a pastor for a short period of my life, but I just couldn't do it right. There was a time when I was an associate pastor of a Presbyterian church in Mount Holly, New Jersey. They had two morning worship services, at 8.30 and 11 a.m. Now, I don't know about you, but I am not wide awake in the mornings. I like to joke around and say that I am a Baptist and Baptists don't believe that God is up at 8.30 in the morning!

Anyway, I was not married at the time, I was still courting. And on Saturday nights – or should I say, Sunday mornings – I would get in much later than a man of God should. One particular Sunday morning, I staggered out of bed and went down to the church to set up for the early morning service. Back then I was responsible for the whole thing except the sermon; the senior pastor had the sermon. I managed to get everything ready and the service got underway at 8.30 a.m. One of the things for which I was responsible was the pastoral prayer.

Now in the Presbyterian church they always end the prayer with this statement: 'We ask all these things in the name of the One who taught us to pray together saying, "Our Father, who art in Heaven, hallowed be Thy name…"' and you know the rest. That morning, I got to the end of the pastoral prayer, and I sleepily said, 'And we ask all these things in the name of the One who taught us to pray together saying,' and before I could catch myself, I heard myself saying, 'Now I lay me down to sleep…' It did not go over well at all!

The worst part of all was that it was Mother's Day. I don't know what it is like at your church, but in that church, Mother's Day is a sentimental orgy. They give out flowers to everybody: to the oldest mother, to the youngest mother (usually the youngest mother is some mother who shouldn't be a mother in the first place – but they give her a flower anyway), to everybody. Then they sing 'Faith of our mothers, living still' – the whole works! It's nice, but that Sunday I couldn't enjoy it because I had just messed up the pastoral prayer.

Before I could recover, it was time for me to read the Scripture. I messed up the Scripture reading, too. The Scripture was 2 Timothy 1, which is about Lois and Eunice, the mother and grandmother of Timothy. Lovely passage for Mother's Day. In my haste, instead of turning to 2 Timothy, the first chapter – you can see this one coming – I turned to 1 Timothy. To say that 1 Timothy, the first chapter, is inappropriate for Mother's Day is putting it mildly.

I mean, picture all those women sitting there with those smug, Mother's Day looks on their faces – and you know how mothers get on Mother's Day (it's enough to make you sick) – listening to me read the wrong passage of Scripture. I read, 'And in the last days there shall be whoremongers, adulteresses, fornicators...' You could just feel the negative vibrations rippling all through the group. The last verse that I read ended, '...and murderers of mothers.' It was shortly after that that I stopped being a Presbyterian and became a Baptist.

Seriously, the institutional church and Christianity deserve a closer look. Sure, there are people who criticize the church. They say it is full of hypocrites. It is. That is why everyone is welcome there. The only difference between the hypocrites inside the church and the hypocrites outside the church is that the hypocrites outside the church don't *know* they are hypocrites.

Everybody is hypocritical. A hypocrite is somebody who does not consistently live out what he believes. I don't consistently live out what I believe. Every day I ask Jesus to make me more consistent with what I believe the Scriptures require me to be. But, to use biblical terminology, 'It has not yet appeared what I shall be.' I am still in the process of becoming the person that Jesus has moulded for me.

To make my point, let's play a game of make-believe. Imagine that you are taking me on a tour of a hospital. You take me through the various wards and show me all the patients. As we come out of the hospital, suppose I say to you, 'I don't like this hospital; everybody in it is sick.' Unfortunately, you would look at me in an incredulous manner and say, 'Of course they are sick. Hospitals are places where sick people come.'

The church of Jesus Christ may have a good number of 'sick' people in it, but thank God they know where to go for help. They know where to go to find healing. Healing the spiritually sick is what church is all about. It proclaims the Word that heals. It offers hope for the troubled. It binds up the hurts of the spiritually wounded.

However, the church is much more than a spiritual hospital. It is also a community of Christians that 'edifies' the saints. In other words, the church teaches and strengthens individual Christians so that each of them can be an effective servant of God in the world.

The apostle Paul teaches that in his letter to the Ephesians, 'And he gave some, apostles; and some, prophets; and some, evangelists; and some, pastors and teachers; For the perfecting of the saints, for the work of the ministry, for the edifying of the body of Christ' (Ephesians 4:11–12).

Some people in your church have the God-given gift of teaching the truths of the Bible. Others may have special prayer powers that bring healing to the sick. Others may have the ability to counsel people, and others may be outstanding preachers. All of these gifted people in the church are called by God to help the members of the church become mature and dynamic Christians who can effectively minister to the needs of people in the world. The Bible teaches us that all of these people have gifts, for the perfecting of the saints for the work of the ministry.

I don't suppose you've ever thought of yourself as a saint before. If you haven't, please let me affirm that you are indeed a saint. According to the Bible, a saint is somebody whom God sets aside to do something special in the church and for the world. That's you! God has something special that He wants you to do for Him. That makes you a saint. If I were you, I wouldn't use the title publicly. I don't think it would go over too big. Nevertheless, it's true. You are called by God to be a saint. So are the other Christians in your church.

The Lord has prepared certain leaders in the church to teach in order to edify the saints by teaching them the Scriptures, to encourage them in spiritual ways and to strengthen them so that they can effectively minister to the world. If the world is going to be reached for Christ, it will be reached through the saints – that's you and me. The people in your school are not coming to church. The people in your neighbourhood are not coming to church. The people at the place where you work are not coming to church. You and I must go to them with the gospel.

The Bible never suggested that they would *come* to the church. Instead, the Bible instructs the church to go to the world. The Bible orders the saints to go into the world and meet people where they live and work and play. We are supposed to tell the people of the world about Jesus as we meet them in the normal course of our daily lives. Jesus commanded us, 'Go into all the world and preach the gospel.' One of the primary purposes of the church is to train and strengthen the saints to do just that. Each of us needs the 'edification' of the church if we are to carry out the great commission of Jesus.

You have a responsibility to build up your church and help it to be and do what Jesus created it to be and do. You could do so much for your church if you would just give yourself and your church a chance. For instance, if your church has a weekly prayer meeting, you could get your whole youth group together and show up. It would be wild if you didn't tell your pastor in advance. You would blow his mind! Have you ever thought of doing that? Or, have you thought of going to a church business meeting to share your beliefs and convictions about how the church can minister to the world? Your church needs your input. If you come in a loving and humble manner, the faithful workers in the church will be thrilled to see you taking an active part in the life of the church. You will be a source of encouragement to everyone.

You need the church and the church desperately needs you. If you do not belong to a church, you have denied yourself one of the major means through which God wants to keep you faithful to him. You are separated from the body of Christ that seeks to prepare you to serve the world.

Get going!

OK, let's review what we've said! (1) Read the Bible. (2) Pray. (3) Start a little support group. Beyond that, (4) be a part of a church and try to make that church into a powerful instrument to equip the saints to do the work of the ministry in the world.

People, this world has to be changed for Jesus. *We've* got to change things and we can do it. We can end poverty for a lot of people. We can end racism in a lot of places. We can bring economic relief and social justice where they are needed. We can lead people to Jesus Christ so that they might become new creatures in Him. We can become people who are strong enough to alter history.

There is enough potential in your home church right now to significantly alter the life of your community and possibly the course of human history. However, if such things are to happen, we've got to make the church into the kind of church that God wants it to be. He does want to change this world and He is expecting you to build His church so that His will might be done on earth as it is in heaven.

You say that the world can't be changed. It is too big, too demonic; it can't be changed or challenged. You're wrong. You and I can do it together. Together with Christ we can build a church that is such a powerful instrument of God that the gates of hell shall not prevail against it.

I belong to a black church in West Philadelphia. I've been a member of that church for decades and for me Mt Carmel Baptist Church is the closest thing to heaven this side of the pearly gates. I preach to a lot of congregations, but I have to say that no other group of people leaves me with excitement like the congregation of my home church. People in my congregation always let me know how I'm doing. Whether I am good or bad, they let me know what they are feeling about my message.

One time when I was preaching, I sensed that nothing was happening. There seemed to be no movement of the dynamism of God. I was struggling, as you have seen ministers struggle, and seemed to be getting nowhere. I had got about three-quarters of the way through my sermon when a lady on the back row yelled, 'Help him, Jesus! Help him, Jesus!' That was all the evidence that I needed that things were not going well that day.

On the other hand, when the preacher is really 'on' in my church, they let him know. The deacons sit right under the pulpit and whenever the preachers says something especially good they cheer him on by yelling, 'Preach, brother! Preach, brother! Preach, man, preach!' And I want to tell you that when they do that to me, it makes me want to preach.

The women in my church have a special way of responding when the preacher is 'doing good.' They usually wave one hand in the air and call out to the preacher, 'Well! Well!' Whenever they do that to me, my hormones bubble.

But that's not all. When I really get going, the men in my congregation shout encouragement by saying, 'Keep going, brother! Keep going! Keep going!' I assure you that a preacher never gets that kind of reaction from a white congregation. White people never yell, 'Keep going! Keep going!' White people are more likely to check their watches and mumble, 'Stop! Stop!'

One Good Friday there were seven of us preaching one after the other, each of us trying to outdo the others. When it was my turn to preach, I rolled into high gear, and I want to tell you, I was good. The more I preached, the more the people in that congregation got 'turned on,' and the more they got 'turned on,' the better I got. I got better and better and better. I got so good that I wanted to take notes on me! At the end of my message, the congregation broke loose. I was absolutely thrilled to hear the hallelujahs and the cries of joy that broke loose throughout the place! I sat down next to my pastor and he looked at me with a smile. He reached down with his hand and squeezed my knee. 'You did all right, boy!' he said. (I must admit that I hate it when he calls me 'boy!')

I turned to him and asked, 'Pastor, are you going to be able to top that?'

The old man smiled at me and he said, 'Son, you just sit back, 'cause this old man is going to do you in!'

I didn't figure that anybody could surpass me that day. I had been so good.... But the old guy got up, and I have to admit, he did me in. The amazing thing was that he did it with the use of one line. For an hour and a half he preached one line over and over again. For an hour and a half he stood that crowd on its ear with just one line. That line was 'It's Friday, but Sunday's comin'!' That statement may not blow you away, but you should have heard him say it. He started his sermon real softly by saying, 'It was Friday. It was Friday, and my Jesus was dead on the tree. But that was Friday, and Sunday's comin'!'

One of the deacons yelled, 'Preach, brother! Preach!' It was all the encouragement that he needed. He came on louder as he said, 'It was Friday, and Mary was cryin' her eyes out. The disciples were runnin' in every direction like sheep without a shepherd, but that was Friday and Sunday's comin'!' People in the congregation were beginning to pick up the message. Women were waving their hands and calling softly, 'Well, well.' Some of the men were yelling, 'Keep going! Keep going!'

The preacher kept going. He picked up the volume still more and shouted, 'It was Friday. The cynics were lookin' at the world and sayin', 'as things have been so they shall be. You can't change anything in this world, you can't change anything.' But those cynics didn't know that it was only Friday. Sunday's comin'!

'It was Friday! And on Friday, those forces that oppress the poor and make the poor to suffer were in control. But that was Friday! Sunday's comin'!

'It was Friday, and on Friday Pilate thought he had washed his hands of a lot of trouble. The Pharisees were struttin' around, laughin' and pokin' each other in the ribs. They thought they were back in charge of things, but they didn't know that it was only Friday! Sunday's comin'!'

He kept on working that one phrase for a half hour, then an hour, then an hour and a quarter, then an hour and a half. Over and over he came at us, 'It's Friday, but Sunday's comin'! It's Friday, but Sunday's comin'! It's Friday, but Sunday's comin'!'

By the time he had come to the end of the message, I was exhausted. He had me and everybody else so worked up that I don't think any of us could have stood it much longer. At the end of his message he just yelled at the top of his lungs, *'It's Friday!'* and all five hundred of us in that church yelled back with one accord, *'Sunday's comin'!'*

Always remember that. Remember that Sunday is coming. Get into the word, pray, form a support group, build up the church, make the church an instrument that will change the world. And though it often seems so dark and dismal, we have the Good News, and the Good News is this: though the world is dark and dismal and demonic, we are going to challenge it, we are going to resist it, we are going to transform it by the grace of God and we will be here to declare the Good News. And the Good News is this: it is Friday, but Sunday's coming!

Over to You

by Denny Rydberg

One of the best ways to really get hold of what Tony
is saying and what you think about what he is saying,
is to spend some time with the material.

A good way to do this is to think specifically about
this book and your own life. To help you do this, we
have put together a series of questions for reflection
and for discussion. And then we've added some action
steps you may want to take.

A suggested plan of attack is this:

First, read the chapter.

Second, spend some time with the reflection questions. Think and write. If you run out of room in the
space provided for each question, write in the margin.
Or better still, begin a journal – and write your
answers there. We suggest using a journal later any-
how, so you may want to start using your journal
here.

Third, get together with some folks and discuss the
group qestions. The group questions are divided into
two sections: 'Getting Started,' and...'Going On.'
The Getting Started ones are designed as warm-up
questions. They let members of a group warm up to
one another and to the topic. Some of the questions

are fairly light. Some are heavier. If you have the time, deal with all the Getting Started questions. If you have little time, take the Getting Started questions you think will most benefit your group. *But don't do away with the Getting Started questions altogether.* It's important to start with questions where almost everyone has an answer, and Getting Started questions do that. Then move to the Going On questions.

Finally, think about the Action activities.

The whole point is to let the material seep into your life and to see if God can use it to touch you and you can use it to touch others. It's that simple.

Now get going!

What is commitment?

REFLECTION – ON YOUR OWN

1. When, if ever, have you tried to 'find yourself'? Did you succeed? Were you helped in the process?
2. How do you feel about Tony's statement. 'There is no such thing as a self waiting to be found...the self is something waiting to be created'?
3. What's the difference between belief and commitment? Can you think of an example from your own life when you believed but weren't committed to something? Describe the situation.
4. What does being committed to Jesus Christ mean to you?
5. How can a person *know* if his or her relationship to Jesus Christ involves real commitment and not just belief?

6. Tony says that being committed to Jesus Christ gives you an identity, a meaning and a purpose to life. How do you feel about what he says? Do you think you're committed to Jesus Christ? If you do, how has Jesus Christ given you an identity, a meaning and a purpose? Be specific.

7. If you were really trying to do what Jesus would do if He was in your situation, how do you think your life would change at home? At school? At work? In your relationship with members of the opposite sex?

8. Tony says the Good News of the Gospel is that when you allow Jesus to come in and possess you, Jesus will do two things. He will enable you to do what you could never do before and He will give you the will to do it. Do you believe this statement? How has Jesus changed your life in these areas?

9. When, if ever, have you experienced the 'joy of Christ'? What factors contributed to your joy? How has Jesus increased the joy in your life?

10. What are some things that really break your heart? How has being a disciple of Jesus Christ increased or decreased your suffering?

11. What makes you angry? How has Jesus influenced your anger?

12. How have you tried to bear another person's burden this week?

13. Does Jesus possess you? If not, why not? What are the reasons for your lack of commitment? What would God need to do for you…what questions would He need to answer before you could give your life to Him?

14. If you are committed, what dream do you have that you'd like to give your life to. If you don't have a dream, would you like one? Explain. How could you go about receiving a 'dream' or a 'vision' from God on something He'd like you to do to change the world for Him?

DISCUSSION – GROUP

Getting Started

1. Who do you know who has taken time off to find himself or herself? What was the result of this person's search?

2. Other than Jesus, who do you think is one of the most committed people who ever lived? Why did you choose that person as an individual who reflects such great commitment?

3. Who is one of the most committed people *you know*? What are the characteristics of his or her life?

4. What are people round you really committed to? What does their commitment 'look' like? How do you know when a person is committed to something?

5. What are some reasons people give for not being committed to Jesus Christ?

6. What are two things that give you a great amount of joy?

7. What are the two things that really make you sad? Angry?

Going On

8. Discuss your thoughts on Reflection question 1. Are the experiences of the group similar? Different? How?

9. Now talk about Reflection question 2. How do you think most people go round trying to 'create self'? How have you tried to create your self in the past? How are you going about it now?

10. Now discuss Reflection questions 3 and 4.

11. Discuss Reflection question 5.

12. Talk about Reflection question 6. How would you answer the reasons that you and the group listed in Discussion question 5? How adept do you feel in answering the objections of people who have rejected a commitment to Jesus Christ? How do you think you

could feel more comfortable?

13. Discuss Reflection question 7.
14. Now Reflection question 8.
15. If you were going to tell a story like Tony's story of Charlie Stoltzfus of God giving you joy in your life, what would the story be? How do you feel if your story doesn't seem as exciting as Tony's?
16. What are some of the things in the world that might 'break God's heart' or anger Him? Make a list. How could you and others join in making a difference in any of these areas?
17. Do Reflection question 11. When is anger good? Bad?
18. Who are three people round you who have significant hurts right now? What could you do in the next week to encourage, comfort or otherwise help them?
19. Do Reflection question 12.
20. Now do Reflection question 14.
21. What have you learned from this chapter? What difference do you hope it makes in your life?

ACTION – ON YOUR OWN

1. For Bible study this week:
   a. Read Luke 19:1–10. Where do you think commitment began for Zacchaeus? How are you and Zacchaeus similar? Different? What do you learn about commitment from this story?
   b. Read John 15:1–11. What does Jesus indicate will contribute to the 'joy' of his disciples? How does this apply to you? What do you think Jesus means by the word *abide*? (*remain* in some versions.) What specific steps could you take this week to more closely abide in Him? Write them down and attempt to take them one step at a time.
   c. Read Romans 12:9–21. In one sentence, what's Paul basic point here? What would be the hardest

thing for you to do of the actions listed here? The easiest? Which one of these traits would you like to work on with God this week?

2. This may be the right time for you to write out a response of commitment to God. If you've never made a commitment to Christ, make it now. If you have already, think it through and write a response that indicates that you 'more than believe'...that you really want to be committed to him.

Dear Jesus...

Signed _____

3. In Discussion question 16, you made a list of things that break God's heart or anger Him. Why not spend some time right now praying that in these areas God's 'will be done on earth as it is in heaven.' Now make a plan. Decide what you can do this week to make a difference. And begin to do it. Keep a journal throughout the week of what you've done and what you've learned as you've pursued this.

4. In Discussion question 13, you thought about people you could reach out to this week. Think of a couple of concrete things that you will do for them. Jot these down. When you've followed them through, put a tick beside them.

Your part in God's revolution

REFLECTION – ON YOUR OWN

1. Who were some of the people who had the greatest effect in sharing Christ with you? How did they witness to you?

2. Before reading this chapter, did you feel you could change the world? Now that you've read it, how do you feel about your ability to make a difference in changing the world?

3. Do you agree with Tony that witnessing for Jesus is the place to begin to change the world? Why or why not?

4. When was the last time you witnessed for Jesus? What happened? How did you feel?

5. What do you think makes Tony good at witnessing? What do you think made Billy good at it? What do you think makes you good at it? How could you improve?

6. What do you see as your 'calling' right now? How do you feel about this calling? How do you think your calling is a witness for Jesus? What kind of witness is it? Explain.

7. How do you think Jesus would handle your calling if He were walking in your shoes? Take a few minutes and imagine Him walking through one of your typical days. How are your ways of dealing with things different from His? How are they the same?

8. How does or has the educational system moulded you? The political system? The business-industrial system? Do you feel you've been made to conform by these systems?

9. How much have you thought about the fact that what you eat influences the living conditions of people in other countries (e.g. Tony's example of how our eating habits create problems for people in the Dominican Republic)? Why or why not? What bad habits would you like to be free of?

10. What particular evil in the world bothers you the most? How would you go about overcoming it? What do you think Jesus would do? If you were to become involved in eradicating this evil, what do you think it

would cost you personally in terms of time, money and commitment? What would it cost you to take the first step? Are you ready to start? Why or why not?

11. What would it take for you to go to the Third World as a missionary? How does the possibility of that make you feel?

DISCUSSION – GROUP

Getting Started

1. What's the most creative and/or humorous way you ever heard of people witnessing for Jesus? How do you feel about that kind of witnessing?

2. If you were king of the world, what are the first two things you would do?

3. What do you think is the world's greatest problem?

4. What do you think are the four most important callings in the world?

5. What would you like to do when you 'grow up'? (Even if you're a senior citizen, this question is for you.)

6. What are five things you really care about?

7. What's your favourite television programme? What are the values that programme conveys? Do you think these values affect you? How? How much?

8. What's the next thing you'd really like to buy?

9. When you think about missionaries, what's the first thing that comes to your mind? How realistic do you think this picture is of missionaries? Explain.

Going On

10. When did Jesus become more than just a name to you? How did it happen? Discuss Reflection question 1 – who were some of the people who shared Christ with you? What are some of the things that Jesus has done in your life since that time? How do you think He's changing you now?

11. Do most people your age believe they can change the world? Why or why not? Discuss your thoughts on Reflection question 2.

12. Discuss Reflection question 5.

13. Who is a person you know who's really using his or her calling for Jesus Christ? How is this witness communicated? What difference does it make?

14. Talk about Reflection question 7.

15. Look again at Discussion question 7. How do you think you and your friends could limit or cancel out the effects the media have on you?

16. What are some other institutions in your life that mould you? Choose one of these institutions as a group and describe some of the ways you are affected by that institution.

17. Think about and discuss Reflection question 9.

18. When, if ever, have you had an experience where the actions of you and a few others changed an institution in some way?

19. Discuss Reflection question 10.

20. Discuss Reflection question 11. Then discuss the questions: How do people you know feel about serving overseas? Why do you think most people would rather stay at home than serve overseas?

21. What's one thing you've learned from this chapter? How would you like your life to change as a result of what you've studied and discussed?

ACTION – ON YOUR OWN

1. For Bible study with week:
   a. Read Romans 1:16–17. How does Paul feel about sharing the gospel with others? How do you feel about the gospel? Can you think of any way in which you might feel ashamed of the gospel? In what ways are you proud of it?

   b. Read Ephesians 6:10–20. Where, if ever, have you had the sense that you were involved in a spiritual battle? What do you think is the meaning of verse 12? What kind of resources has God given you for battle? Which of these resources do you feel you need most right now? Why?

   c. Matthew 5:1–6 and 6:19–34. How do you think Jesus would describe the 'good life'? How does His description compare with yours? If you were to live your life more closely to the values of these Scriptures, how would your life change?

2. Take thirty minutes and go out alone to a place where there's very little noise and have a 'discipline of silence' – thirty minutes with no noise – and think about becoming a revolutionary for God. When you return, jot down some of your thoughts.

3. What's the most difficult thing for you about sharing your faith? Write it down and talk to God about this area all week. Jot down any changes you see as He begins to work in this area of weakness for you. Now make a list of those with whom you'd like to share your faith. Put this list in a spot where you can see it often (but where others can't). Pray for them daily. Take every opportunity God gives you to share. Keep a journal and write down what happens this week in the area of witnessing.

4. How does Tony's challenge to make a difference and change your world feel to you? What is the one thing that you would like to add or subtract from your lifestyle as a result of what you've read in this chapter? What can you do about it this week? Make a plan and carry it out. Tell one person about your plan so that he or she can pray for you and motivate you to stand by it.

5. Fill in the blanks.

    I'll go ....

I'll say ....
I'll do ....
Starting ....
Here's my prayer to be used by you, God:

Boyfriends and girlfriends...and Jesus

REFLECTION – ON YOUR OWN

1. How much have you thought about your Christian commitment in terms of boyfriends or girlfriends. Why or why not?

2. What qualities are you looking for in a boyfriend or girlfriend?

3. What do you think it means to behave right when you go out with your boyfriend or girlfriend? To marry right? Give yourself a mark on how well you have when you go out with your boyfriend or girlfriend. How would you like this to change?

4. When, if ever, have you felt manipulated when you've been out with your boyfriend or girlfriend? How did that make you feel then? How do you feel now as you look back on the experience?

5. If you were having a face-to-face conversation with Jesus about boyfriends and girlfriends, what comments would you make? What questions would you ask?

6. How often did you go out/have you gone out with a boy or girl at school or college? How did/does this affect your self-image?

7. What is Tony's main point when it comes to spirituality and boyfriends/girlfriends?

8. What does a kiss mean to you? What's your view on pre-marital sexual intercourse? What's your view on petting? How consistent are your *views* and your *actions*

when it comes to kissing, sexual intercourse and petting?

9. In twenty-five words or less, what's your definition of love?

10. When, if ever, have you broken up with someone? Who chucked who? How well was it handled? What kind of relationship do you have with that person now? What, if anything, would you have done differently?

11. How much do you want to get married? How much do you want to remain single? Which do you think has the better life – the married person or the single person? Why?

12. What's the hardest part for you in giving your love life over to Jesus and trusting that His way is the best way?

DISCUSSION – GROUP

Getting Started

1. What's one of the most fun experiences of two people going out that you've ever heard about or ever participated in?

2. What's one of the most fun group events you've ever experienced?

3. Who are one of the happiest married couples you've ever known? What do you think makes/made their marriage so great?

4. If you could plan a wedding anyway you'd like to, what would you do?

5. What's one memory you have of a school dance?

6. If you were ruler of the world, would you outlaw having boyfriends and girlfriends? Why or why not?

7. What's one of the best relationships you've ever had (it doesn't have to be a boyfriend/girlfriend relation-

ship or even a relationship with a member of the opposite sex)? What made that relationship so good?

Going On

8. Tony says that there isn't anything that influences your life between the ages of 16–24 more than who you go out with. Do you agree with that? Why or why not?

9. What kind of social pressures do you feel with regard to going out with your boyfriend/girfriend?

10. Have you thought consciously or subconsciously that money spent on going out with someone is an 'investment'?

11. Girls, when you go out with a guy, what do you expect? What do you most appreciate?

12. Guys, when you go out with a girl, what do you expect? What do you most appreciate?

13. How are 'expectations' and 'appreciations' different between the sexes?

14. Why do you think Tony's so opposed to our Western system of going out? What alternatives are there? How do you feel about these alternatives?

15. What would be the end product if people didn't go out with just one person? How practical is the idea of a group of people going out together? Do you think people could really get to know one another? Could they really develop the type of relationship that one needs before marriage? That is, do couples feel more or less in love when they're with a group? Do they tend to develop more or less respect when alone or in a group? Why or why not? How realistic is Tony being? How do you think going out as a group could be put into practice?

16. Discuss Reflection question 5.

17. Discuss Reflection question 7.

18. How can you reach out to people who are lonely and

feeling bad about not having a boyfriend or girlfriend with making it look like a condescending action on your part?

19. How do people around you view sex? What do they think is 'normal'? Why do you think so many young people, including Christians, are involved in pre-marital sex?

20. What have been the major influences in your life that have shaped your view of sex?

21. If you had a Christian friend who was thinking seriously about becoming involved sexually with the person he or she was going out with, what would you tell your friend?

22. Tony says people get hurt when they're involved in pre-marital sex. In what ways can they be hurt? Do men and women get hurt in different ways? Explain. Do you think there are exceptions – are there some people who can emerge without any hurts? Why or why not?

23. Tony talks about love and commitment – looking for someone who has the same commitment as you. How possible is it to find a person like that? And if you could, do you think that a person with the same commitment would make a good spouse? Why or why not?

24. Discuss Reflection question 2.

25. Discuss Reflection question 9.

26. What's the difference between romance and love? What do you think are some of the most important areas to deal with as you get to know someone of the opposite sex in a friendship or as your boyfriend or girlfriend?

27. Discuss Reflection question 14.

28. What's one thing you've learned from this chapter? What difference do you think it will make in your life? What new steps do you want to take as a result of this

chapter? Who could you share your decision with who could help you to follow it through?

ACTION – ON YOUR OWN

1. For Bible study this week:
    a. Read 1 Corinthians 6:12–20. How would Paul respond to a statement like, 'Well, it's my body and I can do what I like with it'? How did you respond to Tony's statement, 'If Jesus is in you, then what you do not only affects you, it affects Jesus, too'?
    b. Read Romans 6:1–2, 18, 22. Why is it illogical and inconsistent for Christians to go on sinning after Christ has saved them? What does it mean when Paul says in verses 18 and 22 that we have been 'set free' from sin? How would your actions change if you realized that Jesus was in the room with you at all times and reading your thoughts at all times? What have you learned from these scriptures that you could apply this week?
    c. Read Ephesians 4:32. What do you think this verse has to do with what Tony said? Define each of the words in this verse by writing their meaning in your own words. Of these qualities, which one do you think you need the most help on? What is one specific way you could work on that quality this week?
2. Write a paragraph about God's gift of sexuality to you. How do you want to treat that gift? What specific actions will you take this week in the area of sexuality? Write them down. Several times this week look at what you've written to see how you're doing.
3. Pay careful attention to the media this week to see how they influence our thinking regarding love, romance, sex and marriage. What are the television programmers communicating? The advertisements?

Magazines, etc? Then work out a plan for how you're going to overcome the media as they attempt to influence you. Try out the plan, make modifications, keep trying. Share what's been happening with a friend.

Priorities in discipleship

REFLECTION – ON YOUR OWN

1. What do you think is the greatest obstacle to your spiritual growth today?

2. How often do you study the Bible each day (each week, each year)? What's your approach to Bible study? What do you usually do?

3. How familiar do you feel with the Bible? How alive does it seem to you?

4. What does Tony say is the secret of the Bible being alive in a person's life? Do you agree with Tony? Why or why not?

5. When, if ever, have you memorized Scripture? What were the results?

6. How much time would you guess you spend a day praying? How important is prayer to you? What usually motivates you to pray more than normal? What things do you usually talk to God about in prayer? What causes you the most difficulty in prayer? How difficult is it for you to be honest with God? Why?

7. When, if ever, has God spoken to you? How did you know it was Him? What did He say? How often does He speak to you?

8. What's the longest time you've ever been silent (and awake)?

9. If God never promises to give you a road-map for direction, how does He expect you to follow His will?

When, if ever, have you wished He'd given you a road-map?

10. Do you have a support group? Do you want one? If you don't have one and want one, what could you do to put one together?

11. When, if ever, have you been corrected by a friend or a group of friends? How did you feel about the correction then? Now?

12. What do you like best about the church? Least about the church? What could you specifically do to make your church a better church?

13. When does it feel like 'Friday' in your life? Would you describe this week as a 'Friday' or a 'Sunday' experience? Why or why not? How does it help to know that 'Sunday's coming'?

14. Tony mentioned four areas which are crucial in maintaining the Christian life: Bible study, prayer, a support group and the church. In which area are you the strongest right now? Which area needs the greatest improvement? What difference do you think it would make in your life if this area were improved? How could you start moving towards this?

DISCUSSION – GROUP

Getting Started

1. What, if any, memories do you have of a special evangelistic service or meeting?

2. What's one of your favourite stories from the Bible?

3. What's one of the greatest answers to prayer you've ever heard about?

4. If you had to be silent for 48 hours, how do you think you would handle it?

5. What's the greatest group you've ever been in? What made it so great?

6. What's one of your fondest memories of the church?

7. If you were the pastor of your local church, how would you change it?

Going On

8. Why do you think so many people who go down the aisle at an evangelistic meeting don't continue in their faith? What traps and detours sidetrack new Christians? Older ones? What traps and detours sidetrack you?

9. What are the greatest barriers for you to consistent, effective Bible study (e.g. lack of discipline, distractions, falling asleep, not being able to understand the text, not knowing where to start, no place to be alone, words don't seem relevant)? Which barriers seem most common to other members of the group? As a group, talk about ways you could overcome these.

10. Discuss Reflection question 5.

11. What does Tony say is the purpose of prayer? Do you agree or disagree with his view? Why or why not?

12. Discuss Reflection question 6.

13. Tony says you need to talk to Jesus 'with intense love and intimacy.' How would you go about doing that? Does this whole thing sound too sweet and sentimental? Why or why not?

14. How do you get your mind quiet enough to hear God? Discuss Reflection question 8 as part of this question.

15. Discuss Reflection 7.

16. Discuss Reflection 9.

17. What are the advantages in having a support group? Disadvantages?

18. Tony says, 'Jesus empowers you through fellowship.' How could this be true?

19. Discuss Reflection question 10.

20. Why is Tony so big on the church? Do you agree with his views? Why or why not?

21. Of the roles Tony says the church fulfils – heals,

equips the saints, provides an opportunity for worship, etc. – what role do you think you need most in your life right now? Why?

22. Draw a 'graph' of your spiritual life and share it with the group. Write in highs and lows and label key events in your spiritual life on the graph. How smooth was your transition from becoming a Christian to becoming involved in a church? What helped the process? Hindered it?

23. Discuss Reflection question 13.

24. Discuss Reflection question 14.

25. When you started reading this book, did you feel a small group of people or an individual could change the world? Have your feelings changed at all? Why or why not?

26. What one thing have you learned from this chapter? How would you like to see your life changed from the input you've received in this chapter?

27. Look back over the whole book. What are two of the most important things you've learned? How is your life different now from when you began studying this book?

ACTION – ON YOUR OWN

1. For Bible study this week:
   Read the Gospel of Mark. To cover it in seven days, you will need to read two chapters a day from Monday to Friday and three a day on Saturday and Sunday. Keep a journal and jot down one significant thing you learn each day. Mark is short. This really won't be an overwhelming assignment.

2. If you've never invited Jesus to take control of your life and you want to, do it now. Just simply say something like, 'Jesus, I believe in you. I want to be committed to you. I want you to come into my life and

possess me. I want you to help me really know you. I want you to know me. I give you my life from this day forth. Thank you.' Believe it: you are filled with His spirit, a new life has begun.

3. Look at what you talked about in Discussion question 9. Think of ways you can apply what you've discussed and begin to put into practice a few of these items this week.

4. Tony says it takes him 20 minutes of silence before be quietens down and can listen to God. Experiment. See how long it takes you to quieten down and hear the voice of God. Spend an increasing amount of time each day in silence until you find that optimal 'quiet-down time' for you.

5. Form a support group. Write down the names of 3–6 people who you think would be interested in a group and begin to talk to them. Find a time and then get together. Agree to meet weekly. At the first meeting, decide the agenda. Do you want to set aside some time for opening up to one another (a must), for prayer, for Bible study? Set the agenda and get going.

6. In prayer, ask God specifically to use you in changing the world. Do this every day and keep your eyes open to opportunities. In your journal, jot down the ways God is changing the world through you.

For further details of Word products please complete coupon below.

Books	☐
Word Records – Cassettes	☐
Lifelifter Cassettes	☐
Video	☐

Please tick items of interest

Name...

Address..

....

....

Word Publishing
Word (UK) Ltd
9 Holdom Avenue, Bletchley, Milton Keynes.
MK1 1QU